MARY GOMES
Food for
Family & Friends

Editor: Melissa Tham
Designer: Lynn Chin
Photographer; Calvin Tan

Published by Marshall Cavendish Cuisine
An imprint of Marshall Cavendish International

Other Marshall Cavendish Offices:
99 White Plains Road, Tarrytown NY 10591-9001, USA • Marshall Cavendish
International (Thailand) Co Ltd. 253 Asoke, 12th Flr, Sukhumvit 21 Road,
Klongtoey Nua, Wattana, Bangkok 10110, Thailand • Marshall Cavendish
(Malaysia) Sdn Bhd, Times Subang, Lot 46, Subang Hi-Tech Industrial Park,
Batu Tiga, 40000 Shah Alam, Selangor Darul Ehsan, Malaysia

Marshall Cavendish is a trademark of Times Publishing Limited

National Library Board, Singapore Cataloguing-in-Publication Data

Names: Gomes, Mary.
Title: Food for family & friends / Mary Gomes.
Other titles: The Eurasian cookbook.
Description: Singapore : Marshall Cavendish Cuisine, [2016] | Includes
    index. | "This book contains previously published material from
    The Eurasian Cookbook."
Identifiers: OCN 933566263 | ISBN 978-981-47-5111-7 (paperback)
Subjects: LCSH: Cooking, Singaporean. | Cooking, Asian.
    | Cooking, European. | Cookbooks.
Classification: LCC TX724.5.S55 | DDC 641.595957--dc23

Printed by Times Offset (M) Sdn Bhd

1944

I would like to dedicate this
book to my late mother, Josephine Gomes
and my late mother-in-law,
Mdm Chua Swee Gek who taught me the
finer points of their cooking skills,
without which I would not have been
able to come up with the recipes for this book.
Not forgetting the late Sister Dorothy Santa Maria
for contributing wonderful recipes to my book which
are retro yet well received by my customers.

Contents

Acknowledgements

I would like to take this opportunity to thank Mr Patrick Mowe for the encouragement given to me to write my first cookbook *The Eurasian Cookbook*. Without his confidence in me, I would not have been able to do it.

He trusted my talent and gave me the encouragement to note down the recipes so that others in the community will benefit from the recipes as well.

During the time when he first approached me, besides advising, he also went a step further to scout for a suitable publisher to take me on although I was a nobody at that time. The odds were great as I had to compete with many renowed authors in the market. Their confidence paid off when my first cookbook was successful and even went into a few reprints.

I thank the Lord for the inspiration enlightened to me when I was doing the book. I never imagined that I could write a successful cookbook.

Preface

I'm glad that *The Eurasian cookbook* was a success. Most of the people who own the cookbook have had nothing but praises for it. Besides the easy-to-follow steps, they find the glossary section very useful as it helps them identify the ingredient needed.

The revised printing undertaken by my new publisher has pictures for every single dish in the book. This will definitely help the cook verify the look of the final product to make a comparison. It also helps that the pictures look very appealing and will definitely pique one's interest when flipping through the cookbook.

I have also included some of the dishes with the complement dishes to go with it, to help you plan the menu you intend to prepare.

As I have compiled a large number of Eurasian recipes, it has been decided that the recipes will be categorised into dishes for everyday cooking and food for family and friends so that its easy when planning for the occasion.

I wish one and all the best of luck and success always.

The Basics

Essentials in a Eurasian Kitchen

CHILLI PASTE

Chilli paste is often used in Eurasian cooking. It is best to make a batch and refrigerate for later use to quicken the cooking process. Store the paste in a clean, dry container and always use a dry spoon to take out the required amount. 2 dried chillies will make about 1 Tbsp chilli paste. However, if you don't cook often, grind the required amount as and when you need it.

30 dried chillies

1. Soak chillies in hot water for about 5 minutes.
2. Grind chillies in an electric blender until fine. Store refrigerated in a clean dry container.
3. The paste will keep for about 1 month.

REMPAHS

Rempahs are herbs and spices ground to a paste. They are used to thicken the gravy of curries, bringing out the taste and sweetening the curry. I find that curries thickened with only curry powder have a bland taste. I use two different *rempahs* in my cooking — basic and standard. They are both made with onions, *belacan*, *buah keras* and chilli but one has *serai* and turmeric powder. I use another *rempah* for vegetable curries. Sufficient oil is required to fry a *rempah* until fragrant. Insufficient oil will turn the *rempah* rancid or mouldy easily. The oil must also be hot enough before the *rempah* is added. This is to prevent it from absorbing too much oil. If the oil is hot enough before the *rempah* is added, the oil will ooze out almost immediately. This can be drained away before the *rempah* is used. You don't need to fry the *rempah* in oil again when using it in your curries.

Basic Rempah

This is used for seafood, chicken and beef. It can be stored in the refrigerator for up to a month if it is fried well. Always use a dry spoon when taking any *rempah* out of the container to prevent the rest of the paste from getting mouldy.

1 kg onions, peeled and cut into chunks

1 Tbsp dried fermented shrimp paste (*belacan*)

20 candlenuts (*buah keras*)

125 ml oil

6 Tbsp ground chilli or 12 dried chillies soaked in hot water and blended until fine

1. Grind onion, *buah keras* and *belacan* together in an electric blender into a fine paste.
2. Heat oil in a wok over medium heat. Fry ground *rempah* until brown.
3. Add ground chilli and fry for 5 minutes until fragrant. Cool.
4. When thoroughly cooled, store in a dry container and refrigerate.

Standard Rempah

This *rempah* has *serai* and turmeric powder and is used for pork, seafood, chicken and vegetables. It can be stored in the refrigerator for up till one month if it is fried well. Always use a dry spoon when taking any *rempah* out of the container to prevent the rest from getting mouldy.

1 kg onions, peeled and cut
   into chunks

2 stalks lemongrass (*serai*)

10 candlenuts (*buah keras*)

1 Tbsp dried fermented shrimp paste (*belacan*)

2 Tbsp ground chilli or 5 dried
   chillies soaked in hot water
   and blended until fine

1 tsp ground turmeric (*kunyit*)

125 ml oil

1. Remove outer layer of *serai*. Slice thinly about 6-cm of the root.

2. Grind onions, *serai*, *belacan* and *buah keras* in an electric blender into a smooth paste.

3. In a bowl, mix with ground chilli and ground *kunyit*. Mix until well blended.

4. Heat oil in a wok over medium heat. Fry ground *rempah* until brown.

5. When thoroughly cooled, store in a dry container and refrigerate.

Vegetable Rempah

1 large onion, peeled and cut into chunks

2 dried chillies

1 tsp dried fermented shrimp paste (*belacan*)

1. Soak chillies in hot water. When softened, blend until fine.

2. Grind onion with *belacan* and ground chilli.

MINCED GARLIC

Another essential of the Eurasian kitchen is minced garlic. If you do a lot of cooking, It's best to grind a batch to store in the refrigerator.

200 g garlic, peeled and washed

1. Mince in an electric blender. Store refrigerated in a clean airtight container (preferably glass as plastic will absorb the smell), or ziplock bags.

2. The minced garlic will keep for about 4–5 days.

SODA BISCUITS

These are square, hard plain biscuits usually sold loosely in local tidbit shops. It is best to keep some ground biscuit crumbs in your pantry for use when you need it. 1 soda biscuit will make about 1 Tbsp biscuit crumbs. If biscuit crumbs are not available, substitute with breadcrumbs.

TAMARIND

To extract tamarind juice

1. Place the required amount of tamarind and water given in the recipe in a bowl.

2. Mix well. Sieve through a strainer for the juice and use as required.

3. Discard the pulp and seeds.

To substitute tamarind juice

Use lime or lemon juice or vinegar.

FENG CURRY POWDER

This mixture is for the quintessential Eurasian dish, *feng*. You can buy the *rempah* from the wet market, or prepare your own. I have given 2 recipes here — one using whole spices and the other using spice powders.

Feng Curry Powder using whole spices

8 Tbsp ground coriander

$^1/_2$ tsp ground cumin (*jintan manis*)

$^1/_2$ tsp ground fennel (*jintan puteh*)

1 tsp ground turmeric (*kunyit*)

1. Wash ground coriander, *jintan manis* and *jintan puteh* under running water. Drain.
2. Dry on a cloth-lined tray in the sun until completely dry.
3. Heat a dry pan. Fry spices over low heat until fragrant. Cool completely.
4. Grind in a mill or coffee grinder until very fine. Add ground turmeric and mix well.
5. Store refrigerated in a dry plastic container. Always use a dry spoon to scoop out the required amount. The curry powder will keep for about 3 months.

Feng Curry Powder using spice powders

8 Tbsp ground coriander

1 tsp ground turmeric (*kunyit*)

$^1/_2$ tsp ground cumin (*jintan manis*)

$^1/_2$ tsp ground fennel (*jintan puteh*)

1. Mix all the spice powders together thoroughly.
2. Store refrigerated in a dry plastic container. Always use a dry spoon to scoop out the required amount. The curry powder will keep for about 3 months.

COCONUT MILK

To extract 240 ml or 300 ml thick coconut milk, use about 450 g grated coconut

1. Rinse a muslin cloth and wring almost, but not completely, dry.
2. Place a handful of grated coconut at a corner of the cloth. Cover the grated coconut with the cloth and squeeze the milk out. Repeat process until all the grated coconut is used.
3. Sieve the milk as there may be some coconut residue.
4. Measure the required amount and use as required.

To extract thin coconut milk

1. Place the squeezed grated coconut after extracting the thick coconut milk in a basin.
2. Add required amount of water and press the grated coconut a few times with your hands. If the quantity of liquid is insufficient, add more water using the same method to extract more milk.
3. Strain through a sieve.
4. Measure the required amount and use as required.

You can also use powdered *santan* or thick coconut milk available in packets.

To substitute coconut milk

Use evaporated, low fat or milk powder for meat/fish curries. If using milk powder, mix 1 Tbsp with 120 ml hot water However, these substitutes cannot be used for *kuehs*.

STOCKS

Pork Stock

This is usually used for noodles.

240 ml water

$1/4$ tsp salt

100 g streaky pork, rinsed

1. Bring water to a boil over low heat.
2. Add salt and pork. Cook for 15 minutes.
3. Strain for later use. Cool and store covered in plastic containers. Store in chiller compartment of the refrigerator. This stock can be kept for 2 days.

Chicken Stock

This stock can also be used as a flavour enhancer for chicken dishes. What I refer to as a 'chicken cage' is the carcass left behind when all the meat is deboned from a whole chicken.

240 ml water

$1/4$ tsp salt

1 chicken cage,
   washed thoroughly

1. Bring water to a boil over low heat.
2. Add salt and chicken bones. Reduce heat, then simmer over low heat for 15 minutes.
3. Strain for use. Cool and store covered in plastic containers. Store in chiller compartment of the refrigerator. This stock can be kept for 2 days.

Beef Stock

This is usually used for tripe *kway teow*.

240 ml water

$1/4$ tsp salt

100 g beef shin, rinsed

1. Bring water to a boil over low heat.
2. Add salt and beef. Reduce heat, then simmer over low heat for 15 minutes.
3. Strain for use. Cool and store covered in plastic containers. Store in chiller compartment of the refrigerator. This stock can be kept for 2 days.

Prawn Stock

This is usually used for noodles or soups.

240 ml water

$1/4$ tsp salt

100 g grey medium-sized
   prawns, washed

1. Bring water to a boil over low heat.
2. Add salt and prawns. Reduce heat, then simmer over low heat for 15 minutes.
3. Strain for use. Cool and store covered in plastic containers. Store in chiller compartment of the refrigerator. This stock can be kept for no more than 2 days.

Cooking Methods

Deep-frying

Usually used for meat or fish. To fry, add enough oil to cover the base of the pan and the item to be fried. Heat oil before frying. Ensure the meat or fish is brown on one side before turning over to brown the other side. Lower the fire to moderately low when the oil is hot. This is to prevent the meat or fish, especially thick fish and pork loins with bones, from burning too fast on the outside whilst the inside is still uncooked.

Stir-frying

Used for cooking vegetables. Sufficient oil is swirled around the pan to ensure the vegetables are crunchy. If green leafy vegetables are used, this method will ensure the vegetables stay green and not turn black.

Shallow Frying

To brown meat fillets or tender cuts of meat or fish. Oil is swirled around the pan till hot before the meat or fish is gently 'slid' in to brown. To prevent meat or fish from sticking to the pan, coat fillets with cornflour.

Simmering

To slow cook a curry or stew, usually with the lid on. It prevents the evaporation of gravy and at the same time tenderises the meat.

Boiling

For soups. Water is brought to boiling point before ingredients are added and cooked till soft.

Pot Roasting or Braising

For roasting meat. The meat is usually marinated with spices and seasoning and water is poured over to just above the meat to tenderise it. This keeps the meat moist while being cooked over low heat. It is basted frequently with the sauce to ensure even browning. The meat is then sliced and served with the rich sauce, topped with peas, onions and fried potatoes.

Weights & Measures

Quantities for this book are given in Metric, Imperial and American (spoon) measures. Standard spoon and cup measurements used are: 1 tsp = 5 ml, 1 Tbsp = 15 ml, 1 cup = 250 ml. All measures are level unless otherwise stated.

LIQUID AND VOLUME MEASURES

Metric	Imperial	American
5 ml	$1/6$ fl oz	1 teaspoon
10 ml	$1/3$ fl oz	1 dessertspoon
15 ml	$1/2$ fl oz	1 tablespoon
60 ml	2 fl oz	$1/4$ cup (4 tablespoons)
85 ml	$2^1/2$ fl oz	$1/3$ cup
90 ml	3 fl oz	$3/8$ cup (6 tablespoons)
125 ml	4 fl oz	$1/2$ cup
180 ml	6 fl oz	$3/4$ cup
250 ml	8 fl oz	1 cup
300 ml	10 fl oz ($1/2$ pint)	$1^1/4$ cups
375 ml	12 fl oz	$1^1/2$ cups
435 ml	14 fl oz	$1^3/4$ cups
500 ml	16 fl oz	2 cups
625 ml	20 fl oz (1 pint)	$2^1/2$ cups
750 ml	24 fl oz ($1^1/5$ pints)	3 cups
1 litre	32 fl oz ($1^3/5$ pints)	4 cups
1.25 litres	40 fl oz (2 pints)	5 cups
1.5 litres	48 fl oz ($2^2/5$ pints)	6 cups
2.5 litres	80 fl oz (4 pints)	10 cups

DRY MEASURES

Metric	Imperial
30 grams	1 ounce
45 grams	$1^1/2$ ounces
55 grams	2 ounces
70 grams	$2^1/2$ ounces
85 grams	3 ounces
100 grams	$3^1/2$ ounces
110 grams	4 ounces
125 grams	$4^1/2$ ounces
140 grams	5 ounces
280 grams	10 ounces
450 grams	16 ounces (1 pound)
500 grams	1 pound, $1^1/2$ ounces
700 grams	$1^1/2$ pounds
800 grams	$1^1/2$ pounds
1 kilogram	2 pounds, 3 ounces
1.5 kilograms	3 pounds, $4^1/2$ ounces
2 kilograms	4 pounds, 6 ounces

OVEN TEMPERATURE

	°C	°F	Gas Regulo
Very slow	120	250	1
Slow	150	300	2
Moderately slow	160	325	3
Moderate	180	350	4
Moderately hot	190/200	375/400	5/6
Hot	210/220	410/425	6/7
Very hot	230	450	8
Super hot	250/290	475/550	9/10

LENGTH

Metric	Imperial
0.5 cm	$1/4$ inch
1 cm	$1/2$ inch
1.5 cm	$3/4$ inch
2.5 cm	1 inch

Soups and Stews

Teem with Pig's Trotters *18*

Babi Pongteh *20*

Beef Smore *21*

Mulligatawny soup *22*

Pork Ribs Stew *25*

Teem With Pig's Trotter

This is served for supper after midnight mass. The soup is usually heated till piping hot before serving. As *kiam chye* is salty, do not add salt till you've tasted the soup. Serve with French loaf and dipping sauce.

Serves 4–6

200 g salted preserved mustard (*kiam chye*), stems only, rinsed and cut into 8–10 big pieces

1 pig's trotter, about 600–700 g, cut into large pieces and discard toes

2 pieces preserved plum (*kiam buay*), rinsed

100 g black beans, rinsed

1 bunch (5–6 cloves) garlic, do not separate

240 ml water

1 tsp sugar

1 Tbsp brandy

Dipping Sauce

4 Tbsp dark soy sauce

2 red chillies, sliced

1. Soak *kiam chye* overnight to drain excess salt. Change water a few times.

2. Wash and drain pig's trotter.

3. Place trotter in a medium-sized pot.

4. Add *kiam chye*, *kiam buay*, black beans and garlic.

5. Add water and bring to a boil over low heat.

6. Add sugar and brandy. Lower heat, then simmer for about 45 minutes until meat is tender and beans and *kiam chye* are soft.

7. Prepare dipping sauce. Mix well and serve with pig's trotter.

Babi Pongteh

The consistency of the gravy is important. It must be thick enough and is served best with sambal *belacan*.

Serves 4–6

3 onions, peeled and sliced

5 cloves garlic, peeled

2 Tbsp oil

10-cm cinnamon, washed

1 Tbsp preserved soybeans (*taucheo*)

1 pig's trotter or 300 g lean pork
  (*twee bak*), cut into pieces,
  washed then drained

2 Tbsp dark soy sauce

2 Tbsp sugar

$^1/_2$ Tbsp salt

720 ml water

300 g yam bean (*bang kwang*),
  peeled and cut into wedges

4 potatoes, peeled and cut into
  quarters then soak in water

a sprig of coriander (*ketumbar*)

1. Blend onions and garlic in a blender or a food processor until fine.

2. Heat oil in a pot over medium heat. Fry cinnamon, ground onions and garlic until light brown and fragrant.

3. Add *taucheo* and fry for 1 minute.

4. Add pork pieces and stir-fry for 3 minutes.

5. Add dark soy sauce, sugar, salt and water.

6. When meat is half-cooked, add *bang kwang*. Cover lid and cook for 15 minutes.

7. Add potatoes and cook until meat is tender, *bang kwang* is soft, potatoes are cooked and stew thickens.

8. Dish out and serve. Garnish with coriander leaves.

Beef Smore

When it comes to Beef Smore, I'm particular that I use beef shank as the tendons melt in your mouth when they are done well.

Serves 4–6

300 g beef shank, cut into 2.5-cm pieces, rinsed then drained

$^1/_4$ tsp bicarbonate of soda

2 Tbsp ground black pepper

1 tsp salt

1 tsp sugar

2 Tbsp vinegar

4 Tbsp dark soy sauce

2 onions, peeled and sliced

5 cloves garlic, peeled and sliced

100 g small carrots, peeled and diagonally sliced

3 potatoes, peeled and quartered

2 Tbsp oil

1 thumb-sized piece ginger, peeled and julienned

10-cm cinnamon, washed

420 ml water

1 tomato, quartered

2 soda biscuits, crushed and ground

1 tin luncheon meat or chicken frankfurters (optional)

a sprig of coriander (*ketumbar*)

1. In a bowl, marinate beef with bicarbonate of soda, ground black pepper, salt, sugar, vinegar and dark soy sauce for 30 minutes.

2. Grind onions and garlic together in a blender or a food processor until fine.

3. Soak julienned carrots and potatoes together.

4. Heat oil in a pot over medium heat. Fry ground onion and garlic, julienned ginger and cinnamon until onions are caramelised and fragrant.

5. Add marinated beef. Fry until meat changes colour.

6. Add water and simmer until meat is tender. Stir occasionally to prevent meat from sticking to pot. Add more water if gravy is too thick and season accordingly.

7. Add carrots and cook for 5 minutes.

8. Add potatoes and cook until soft.

9. Add tomato, biscuit crumb and luncheon meat or chicken franks, if using.

10. Garnish with coriander leaves.

Mulligatawny Soup

This is traditionally served after midnight mass as it is light enough for supper. Serve with French loaf.

Serves 4–6

6 Tbsp coriander seeds

2 tsp fennel (*jintan puteh*)

1 tsp cumin (*jintan manis*)

2–3 dried chillies, soaked in hot water

2 Tbsp black peppercorns

210 ml water

1 Tbsp mustard seeds, washed

1 Tbsp cumin seeds, washed

2 pieces chicken breast with bone, washed

2 walnut-sized pieces tamarind (*assam*), mixed with 60 ml water and strained.

1 thumb-sized piece ginger, smashed

5-cm piece dry turmeric (*kunyit*), smashed

60 ml thin coconut milk

1 Tbsp salt

2 tsp oil

10 shallots, peeled and sliced

6 cloves garlic, peeled and sliced

2 sprigs curry leaves (*daun kari*)

1. Grind coriander, *jintan puteh*, *jintan manis*, dried chillies and black peppercorns until fine.

2. Bring ground spices and water to a boil in a pot over low heat. Lower heat, then simmer until spice stock is reduced to two-thirds of original volume. Strain.

3. Add mustard seeds, cumin seeds and chicken to stock. Bring back to a boil over low heat. Lower heat, then simmer until meat softens.

4. Add *assam* water, ginger, turmeric, coconut milk and salt.

5. When meat is tender, remove from stock. Set aside to cool before shredding.

6. Keep stock at a simmer.

7. In a pan, heat oil over medium heat. Fry shallots, garlic and curry leaves until shallots and garlic are golden brown. Add to stock.

8. Place some shredded chicken in a bowl. Heat soup until piping hot and pour over chicken.

9. Serve.

Pork Ribs Stew

The fragrance of this soup is uniquely Eurasian. It is almost always served if there are any children at a family gathering. Serve with rice, sambal *belacan* or *timun* (page 91), fried meatballs or corned beef cutlets and fried brinjals (page 72).

Serves 4–6

300 g spareribs or minced pork
    or chicken

2 tsp ground black pepper

2 tsp salt

2 tsp sugar

$\frac{1}{4}$ tsp dark soy sauce

oil, as needed

2 potatoes, peeled and quartered

2 chicken frankfurters or $\frac{1}{2}$ tin
    luncheon meat, washed

1 onion, peeled and quartered

2 cloves

2.5-cm cinnamon

420 ml water

1 carrot, peeled and diagonally cut

4 cabbage leaves, cut into 4 pieces each
    and washed

2 soda biscuits, crushed and ground

a sprig of coriander (*ketumbar*),
    washed and cut into 5-cm lengths

1. Wash and drain spareribs. Marinate with 1 tsp ground black pepper, 1 tsp salt, 1 tsp sugar and dark soy sauce for 20 minutes.

2. If using minced pork or chicken, marinate with seasonings, 1 beaten egg and 2–3 tsp ground biscuit or breadcrumbs. Mix well and form into small balls, each about 20 g. Lightly fry in oil.

3. Shallow fry potatoes until brown.

4. Cut each chicken frank into 3. If using luncheon meat, halve and then cut into 4.

5. Heat 1 Tbsp oil in a pot over medium heat. Fry onion, cloves and cinnamon until fragrant and onion is soft.

6. Add marinated spareribs or fried meatballs and fry until meat changes colour.

7. Add 420 ml water, remaining salt, sugar and ground black pepper. Simmer over low heat for about 30 minutes until meat is tender.

8. Add carrot. Cook for 5 minutes.

9. Add cabbage and potatoes. Cook until soft.

10. Add luncheon meat or chicken franks and biscuit crumbs. If stew is too thick, add a little more water for desired consistency.

11. Garnish with coriander.

12. Dish out and serve.

Poultry

Chicken Buah Keluak 28

Curry Debal 31

Chicken Chilli Curry 32

Chicken Soy Limang 33

Chicken Capitan 34

Eurasian Chicken Pie 36

Chicken Buah Keluak

When I was young, my mum used to tell me how her neighbours in Malacca used to prepare the Tok Panjang, a Peranakan custom of serving food on a long (*panjang*) table for special occasions. This dish was always prepared one day before as it tastes best when kept overnight. If you like your curry thick, add more *rempah* and adjust the seasonings accordingly. Serve with rice and fried and salted/fresh fish, or salted eggs.

Serves 4–6

20 Indonesian black nuts (*buah keluak*)

6 chicken wings, cut into 2 pieces, then washed and drained

$^1/_2$ tsp salt

2 walnut-sized pieces tamarind (*assam*), mixed with 120 ml water and strained

4 Tbsp standard *rempah* (see page 11)

480 ml water

1 tsp salt

2 tsp sugar

1. Soak *buah keluak* in water overnight. The next day, brush the shells to remove any sand or sediment. Rinse a few times until water runs clear. Crack each nut with a small hammer on the flat surface.

2. Marinate chicken with salt.

3. Heat a deep pot over medium heat. Add *rempah*. Fry for 1–2 minutes or until oil oozes out.

4. Add marinated chicken and *buah keluak*. Fry for 5 minutes over high heat.

5. Lower heat. Add water, salt, sugar and *assam* water. Bring to a boil over low heat.

6. When curry boils, lower heat and simmer until meat is tender and gravy thickens.

7. Dish out and serve.

Curry Debal

This is the curry most associated with Eurasians. It is cooked for special occasions like Christmas or any other big festivity. The curry can be kept for about a week, if you do not add the vegetables at Step 4. For a thicker curry, use more onions. Serve with rice or French loaf and corned beef cutlets and fried brinjals (page 72).

Serves 4–6

1 kg chicken, cut into bite-sized pieces, washed then drained

1 tsp ground black pepper

2 tsp salt

2 tsp sugar

1/4 tsp dark soy sauce

4 potatoes, peeled and quartered

1 cucumber, washed and cut into 3–4 segments

3 Tbsp oil

6 onions, peeled and ground

1 thumb-sized piece ginger, peeled and julienned

1 tsp mustard seeds or 1/2 tsp mustard powder

2–3 Tbsp ground chilli

360 ml water

4 cabbage leaves, cut into bite-sized pieces

1/2 tin luncheon meat or 5 chicken frankfurters (optional), cut into 7.5 x 2.5-cm pieces

100 g *babi panggang* (optional), cut into 5-cm thick slices

2 Tbsp vinegar

1. Marinate chicken with ground black pepper, 1 tsp salt, 1 tsp sugar and dark soy sauce. Mix well and leave to stand for 20 minutes.

2. Soak potatoes in water.

3. Cut each segment of cucumber into 4. Remove seeds.

4. Heat oil in a wok over medium heat. Drain potatoes and fry until golden brown. Place in a medium-sized pot.

5. In the same oil, fry chicken until brown. Place in pot with potatoes.

6. Retain 3 Tbsp oil in wok. Fry onions and ginger until brown.

7. Add mustard seeds or powder and ground chilli. Fry for 5 minutes. Add to pot with chicken and potatoes.

8. Add water, salt and sugar. Bring to a boil over low heat. Lower heat, then simmer for 5 minutes.

9. Add cabbage and cucumber. Cook for about 10 minutes until vegetables are tender.

10. Add luncheon meat or chicken franks and *babi panggang*, if using.

11. Add vinegar. Bring back to a boil.

12. Remove from heat.

13. Dish out and serve.

Chicken Chilli Curry

I love eating this coconut-based curry with French Loaf.

Serves 4–6

1 chicken, about 1 kg, cut into bite-sized pieces, washed then drained

3 tsp salt

4 potatoes, peeled and quartered

3 large onions, peeled

5 cloves garlic, peeled

1 thumb-sized piece ginger, peeled

3 Tbsp oil

7-cm cinnamon

4 cardamoms, washed then crush slightly

1–2 Tbsp ground chilli

2 Tbsp meat curry powder

2 tsp sugar

720 ml water

1 tomato, quartered

240 ml thick coconut milk

1. Marinate chicken with 1 tsp salt.

2. Wash and soak potatoes in water.

3. Grind onions, garlic and ginger in a blender or a food processor until fine.

4. Heat oil in a pot over medium heat. Add cinnamon, cardamoms and ground ingredients. Fry until fragrant and brown.

5. Add ground chilli and curry powder. Fry for 2 minutes.

6. Add chicken. Stir-fry until chicken changes colour.

7. Add potatoes, salt and sugar.

8. Add water and bring to a boil over low heat. Lower heat, then simmer until meat and potatoes are soft.

9. Add tomato and coconut milk. Bring back to a boil.

10. Remove from heat.

11. Dish out and serve.

Chicken Soy Limang

This Eurasian fried chicken is usually served for special occasions like Christmas and birthdays. Fry the potato slices first, as the chips will have specks of black dots if fried in used oil. Serve with rice and any meat curry or meatball stew.

Serves 4–6

1 chicken, about 1 kg, cut into bite-sized
    pieces, washed then drained

1 tsp ground black pepper

1/2 tsp dark soy sauce

1 tsp salt

1 tsp sugar

2 potatoes, peeled, washed then
    thinly sliced

120 ml oil

1 onion, peeled and cut into rings

1 tomato, sliced into thin rounds

2 Tbsp frozen green peas

60 ml water

4 Tbsp dark soy sauce

2 tsp plum sauce

3 limes, halved and squeezed

1. Marinate chicken with ground black pepper, dark soy sauce, salt and sugar. Mix well and leave to stand for 30 minutes.

2. Heat oil in a wok over medium heat. Fry potatoes until golden brown. Remove from wok. Transfer to a plate lined with kitchen towels.

3. In the same oil, deep-fry chicken until golden brown. Drain and arrange neatly on serving dish.

4. Blanch onion rings in boiling water for 3 minutes. Drain.

5. Wash tomato. Slice thinly into rounds.

6. Blanch green peas in boiling water for 1 minute. Drain.

7. Mix water, dark soy sauce and plum sauce in a shallow pot. Bring to a boil over low heat.

8. Add lime juice.

9. Pour gravy evenly over fried chicken.

10. Garnish with onion rings, tomatoes, green peas and top with fried potato chips.

Chicken Capitan

This is an essential dish for special occasions, like birthdays, anniversaries and christenings. For a thicker curry, use more onions. Serve with rice or French loaf, fried corned beef cutlets and fried brinjals (page 72).

Serves 4–6

1 chicken, about 1 kg, cut into bite-sized
   pieces, washed then drained

2 tsp salt

1 tsp sugar

1 tsp ground black pepper

$^1/_2$ tsp dark soy sauce

4 potatoes, peeled and quartered

5–6 large onions, peeled

250 ml oil

$^1/_2$ tsp mustard paste or powder

2–3 Tbsp ground chilli

420 ml water

3 chicken frankfurters, cut into
   3 pieces each (optional)

4–5 limes, cut and squeezed

1. Marinate chicken with 1 tsp salt, 1 tsp sugar, ground black pepper and dark soy sauce. Mix well and leave for 20 minutes.

2. Wash and soak potatoes in water.

3. Grind onions in a blender or a food processor until fine.

4. Heat oil in a wok over medium heat. Drain potatoes and fry until golden brown. Remove from heat. Place in a deep pot.

5. In the same oil, fry chicken pieces until brown. Remove from heat. Place in pot with potatoes.

6. Retain 3 Tbsp oil in wok. Fry ground onions until brown.

7. Add mustard paste or powder and ground chilli. Fry for 2 minutes. Transfer fried *rempah* into pot with chicken and potatoes.

8. Add water, salt and sugar. Simmer for 5 minutes.

9. Add chicken franks, if using. Cook until meat and potatoes are tender.

10. Add lime juice. Bring to a boil over low heat.

11. Dish out and serve.

Eurasian Chicken Pie

Traditionally, in Eurasian homes, gifts are exchanged after midnight mass on Christmas Day. This chicken pie, with its unique filling of chicken, meatballs, sausages, boiled eggs, potatoes, carrots and peas, is often served at the reunion supper that follows.

Makes one 30 x 15-cm pie

1 egg, beaten

Pastry

500 g plain (all-purpose) flour

1 tsp baking powder

1 egg

1/4 tsp salt

2–3 Tbsp boiled water

250 g softened butter

Filling

1 kg chicken fillet, skin removed and cut into bite-sized pieces

4 tsp ground black pepper

3 tsp salt

3 tsp sugar

1/4 tsp dark soy sauce

6 soda biscuits, crushed and ground

200 g minced pork

1 egg

3 potatoes, peeled and cut into 8 pieces each then soak in water

2 carrots, peeled and cut diagonally into 5-mm pieces

5–6 chicken frankfurters, washed and cut into 3 pieces each

1 onion, peeled and quartered

3-cm cinnamon

2–3 cloves

2 Tbsp green peas

6 hard-boiled eggs, shelled and cut into wedges

2 sprigs spring onions (scallions), washed and cut into 3-cm lengths

125 ml oil

720 ml water

1. Prepare pastry. Sift flour and baking powder into a basin.

2. Add egg and mix until mixture resembles breadcrumbs.

3. Mix salt with water. Pour into flour mixture. Mix well.

4. Rub in softened butter. Mix until a firm dough is formed. Leave to stand for 5 hours, or overnight at room temperature.

5. Prepare filling. In a bowl, marinate chicken with 1 tsp ground black pepper, 1 tsp salt, 1 tsp sugar and dark soy sauce. Set aside for 10 minutes.

6. Mix minced meat with egg, 1 tsp ground black pepper, 1 tsp salt, 1 tsp sugar and 2 Tbsp biscuit crumbs. Mix thoroughly. Pinch and form into small balls.

7. Blanch green peas in hot water for 1 minute.

8. Heat oil in a wok over medium heat. When hot, fry potatoes until light brown. Remove and drain.

9. Fry meatballs until light brown. Remove and drain. Set aside with potatoes.

10. Fry marinated chicken until brown. Remove and drain. Set aside with potatoes and meatballs.

11. Reserve 1 Tbsp oil in wok. Fry onion, cinnamon, cloves and carrots until onion softens.

12. Add water, 1 tsp salt, 1 tsp sugar and 2 tsp ground black pepper. Simmer until carrots are soft.

13. Add chicken, meatballs, potatoes and chicken frankfurters. Cook until meat is soft.

14. Add remaining biscuit crumbs to thicken gravy. When gravy comes to a boil, remove from heat.

15. Cool completely and strain. Set gravy aside.

16. Preheat oven to 200°C.

17. Fill a 30 x 15-cm rectangular glass or enamel pie dish with the strained cooked meat and vegetables.

18. Place egg wedges evenly on top. Garnish with spring onions and green peas.

19. Place half the dough on a plastic sheet. Cover with another plastic sheet. Flatten with a rolling pin into a piece big enough to cover the pie dish, about 1.5-cm thick.

20. Remove plastic sheet. Lift pastry up carefully and cover filling in the pie dish with dough. Trim the sides by running a knife over the side of the dish.

21. Using the same method as above, roll the rest of the pastry to about 1.5-cm thick.

22. Cut to form a square sheet. Using a sharp knife, cut dough into 3.5-cm thick strips.

23. Tape the edge of the pie dish with the strips.

24. Roll the remaining dough and flatten again into a piece about 1.5-cm thick. Cut into 1.5-cm strips. Criss-cross the strips over the surface of the pie.

25. Use a dough pincher and pinch designs on the dough to enhance the appearance of the dough.

26. Brush egg wash on surface of pie. Bake in oven at 200°C for about 20–30 minutes until pie is golden brown.

27. To serve, heat gravy until hot. Cut a square of pastry out at the side of the pie and pour some of the gravy in.

28. Serve pie with gravy.

Meat

Honey Baked Ham *40*

Pattie Curry Puffs *42*

Vindaloo *43*

Curry Feng *44*

Pang Susie *46*

Belimbing Beef Curry *47*

Beef Curry *49*

Pot Roast Beef *50*

Seh Bak *53*

Shepherd's Pie *54*

Mutton Chop Curry Moru *57*

Honey Baked Ham

In our family, it only feels like Christmas when Honey Baked Ham is scrved!
This is a must-have for our Christmas gatherings and parties.

Serves 4–6

1.4 kg gammon ham

water, as needed

1 can (323 ml) beer

4 star anise

3-cm piece cinnamon

10 cloves

2 Tbsp sugar

cloves, as needed

pineapple slices, as needed

Glaze

2 Tbsp brown sugar

2 Tbsp honey

1 tsp mustard

juice from 1 orange

1. Boil ham in a big pot of water with beer, star anise, cinnamon, cloves and sugar for 1–1.5 hours until meat is cooked and tender.

2. Set aside to cool for 1 hour.

3. Drain meat and transfer to a roasting pan.

4. Preheat oven to 175°.

5. Prepare glaze. Mix brown sugar, honey, mustard and orange juice in a bowl. Slowly stir until sugar dissolves.

6. Remove skin from ham. Using a very sharp knife, score ham and make diamond patterns.

7. Brush ham with glaze. Insert cloves into corners of diamonds.

8. Bake at 175°C for 20 minutes

9. Remove baking pan from oven. Arrange pineapple slices around ham. Return pan to oven and bake for a further 10 minutes until golden brown. Baste meat occasionally with gravy from the pan.

10. Cool and chill in refrigerator. The ham has to be served cold.

Pattie Curry Puffs

These patties will look flat if not enough filling is used. However if too much is used, the filling will ooze out of the patty. Use your discretion well!

Makes 30 curry puffs

1 egg, beaten

Pastry
500 g plain (all-purpose) flour

1 tsp baking powder

1 egg

pinch of salt

3 Tbsp boiled water

250 g softened butter

Filling
200 g potatoes, peeled and diced
    into 1-cm cubes then soaked in water

1 Tbsp oil

1 onion, peeled and diced

1 tsp minced garlic

1 tsp minced ginger

300 g minced pork, chicken or beef

1 tsp salt

2 tsp sugar

2–3 Tbsp meat curry powder

120 ml water

1. Prepare pastry, Sift flour and baking powder into a mixing bowl.

2. Add egg to flour mixture. Mix with fingertips.

3. Dissolve salt in water. Add to flour mixture and mix well.

4. Rub in butter until a well-mixed dough is formed. Leave to stand at room temperature for 5 hours or overnight.

5. Prepare filling. Heat oil in a pan over medium heat. When hot, fry diced onion, garlic and ginger until onion softens.

6. Drain potatoes and add to pan. Stir-fry for 1 minute. Add minced meat, salt and sugar. Mix thoroughly.

7. Add curry powder. Fry over low heat until mixture is well mixed.

8. Add water. Simmer until meat and potatoes are cooked and mixture is dry. Remove from heat and set aside to cool completely.

9. Preheat oven to 200°C. Line baking tray with baking paper. Set aside.

10. Place dough on a plastic sheet. Cover with another plastic sheet. Flatten with a rolling pin until pastry is about 0.5-cm thick.

11. Remove top plastic sheet. Using a 5-cm round pastry cutter, cut circles of pastry out.

12. Remove cut pastry circles. Press edges lightly to thin out the pastry and make filling it easier.

13. Place 1 Tbsp filling on pastry circle. Cover with another circle. Make sure edges are sealed. Using a dough pincher, pinch sides to make a pattern.

14. Place patties on prepared baking tray about 5-cm apart to prevent patties from sticking together.

15. Brush surface of patties with egg wash.

16. Bake in oven at 200°C for 20–30 minutes until patties are golden brown.

Vindaloo

This curry should be dry. Do not add any water if using chicken, but add a little if pork is used.

Serves 4–6

1 kg pork or chicken, cut into bite-sized
    pieces, washed then drained

2 onions, peeled; 1 sliced

1 thumb-sized piece ginger, peeled

3 cloves garlic, peeled

3 Tbsp vindaloo curry powder

2 Tbsp oil

1 Tbsp light soy sauce

1–2 tsp sugar

1 Tbsp vinegar

1. Grind onion, ginger and garlic in a blender or a food processor until fine.

2. Marinate meat with ground ingredients and curry powder. Set aside for 10 minutes.

3. Heat oil in a pot over medium heat. Sauté sliced onion until soft.

4. Add marinated meat, light soy sauce and sugar. Cover with lid and cook over low heat until meat is tender.

5. Add vinegar. Stir to mix well and remove from heat.

6. Dish out and serve.

Curry Feng

This is a Christmas specialty which is best eaten a day old. A big pot of it is normally cooked as it is a tedious process preparing this dish. To keep the curry longer, cool completely before freezing. Reheat the required amount as and when required. This way the curry will taste just as good as a freshly cooked one. It will also not get dry with numerous reheatings. The pork can be substituted with chicken fillet and liver. The *feng* curry powder can be purchased from the *rempah* stalls at most Singapore wet markets. Just ask the *rempah* man to blend *jintan* manis, *jintan puteh*, *ketumbar* and *kunyit*.

Serves 4–6

200 g lean pork (*twee bak*)

100 g pork belly, washed and drained

30 pig's liver, washed and drained

3 large onions, peeled

3 cloves garlic, peeled

1 thumb-sized piece ginger, peeled
   and julienned

2.5-cm cinnamon, washed

2–3 Tbsp oil

3 Tbsp *feng* curry powder
   (see page 12)

2 tsp salt

1 tsp sugar

2 Tbsp vinegar

1. Parboil pork and liver until colour changes. Remove meat from water and cool. Dice into small cubes. Strain water and reserve 420 ml for later use.

2. Grind onions and garlic together in blender or a food processor until fine.

3. Heat a pot. When hot, add oil and fry onions, garlic, ginger and cinnamon until light brown and fragrant.

4. Add diced pork and liver and fry for 5 minutes to melt fat from pork.

5. Add curry powder, salt and sugar. Stir-fry for 2 minutes.

6. Add water and simmer until meat is soft and gravy thickens.

7. Add vinegar. Bring to a boil over low heat.

8. Remove from heat.

9. Dish out and serve.

Pang Susie

The dough of the authentic Eurasian Susie bun or *pang* is made of sweet potatoes, yeast, eggs, butter, flour and milk. Different cooks make their *pang susies* in different sizes— from petite to large. Remember, the smaller ones are quicker to bake. Store *pang susies* in the refrigerator. Reheat in the oven or microwave as and when required.

Makes 30 small buns

1 egg yolk, lightly whisked

Dough
2 large sweet potatoes, peeled

300 g plain (all-purpose) flour

1$\frac{1}{2}$ tsp dry yeast

70 g sugar

100 g butter

1 egg yolk

2 Tbsp evaporated milk

2 Tbsp brandy

Filling
400 g minced pork

$\frac{1}{2}$ tsp clove powder

$\frac{1}{2}$ tsp cinnamon powder

$\frac{1}{2}$ tsp nutmeg powder

200 g onions, peeled and finely diced

2 Tbsp oil

1 Tbsp sugar

1 tsp dark soy sauce

$\frac{1}{2}$ Tbsp salt

1. Prepare dough. Boil sweet potatoes until tender. Drain and mash with a fork until smooth. Remove fibres, if there are any. Measure 200 g and set aside.

2. Sift flour with yeast into a mixing bowl. Add sugar and mix thoroughly.

3. Add butter and rub with finger tips until mixture resembles fine breadcrumbs.

4. Add egg yolk, evaporated milk, brandy and mashed sweet potato. Mix thoroughly until mixture is smooth and a soft dough forms.

5. Shape dough into a round ball. Cover bowl with a damp cloth and set aside at room temperature for 30 minutes.

6. Prepare filling. Marinate meat with clove, cinnamon and nutmeg powders. Leave aside for 10 minutes.

7. Heat oil in a pan over medium heat. When hot, fry onions for about 4–5 minutes until slightly browned.

8. Add marinated meat, sugar, dark soy sauce and salt. Stir-fry until meat is cooked and filling is dry. Cool completely.

9. Preheat oven to 180°C. Line baking trays with baking paper. Set aside.

10. Portion dough into small balls, each about 50 g.

11. Flatten dough on a floured surface.

12. Place 1 Tbsp filling in the centre of the dough. Draw up edges to seal. Shape buns so that the ends taper like a rugby ball. Place on prepared baking trays.

13. Brush each bun with egg wash. Set aside leftover egg.

14. Bake in oven at 180°C for 25 minutes or until buns are golden brown.

15. Remove from oven immediately and while hot, brush surface with remaining egg wash.

16. Allow *pang susie* to cool down before serving.

Belimbing Beef Curry

As *belimbing* is seasonal, wherever there's plentiful in the market, we will take the opportunity to make as many variations we can think of to make use of the fruit. Serve with rice or French loaf and fried salted fish or salted eggs, and sambal *timun* (page 91) or sambal *nanas* (page 88).

Serves 4–6

300 g beef fillet, washed and drained

¼ tsp bicarbonate of soda

4 Tbsp standard *rempah (see page 11)*

4–5 sour starfruits (*belimbing*), cut into rounds

1 tsp salt

2 tsp sugar

240 ml water

120 ml thick coconut milk

1. Pat dry beef fillet and slice. Marinate with bicarbonate of soda and set aside for 10 minutes.

2. Heat a pan over medium heat. Add *rempah*. Fry for 1 minute.

3. Add *belimbing* and continue frying.

4. Add beef, salt, sugar and water. Simmer until meat is tender.

5. Add thick coconut milk and bring to a boil over low heat. When gravy boils, remove from heat.

6. Dish out and serve.

Pang Susie

Belimbing Beef Curry

Beef Curry

This has been nicknamed 'Maundy Thursday Beef Curry' by my friend, Patrick Mowe. His brother-in-law first discovered it when he visited my church, St. Joseph's on Victoria Street, on a Maundy Thursday. Ever since then, Patrick has been organising small Sunday lunches at the church with his 'kakis'. He'll call me a week in advance to let me know what they want and he'll always ask for the beef curry. Sometimes he'll even ask for a little extra to take home. On one occasion, a guest of Patrick's from Australia was so impressed that he asked if I'd like to be a guest cook at his daughter's restaurant in Perth!

Serves 4–6

500 g beef shank, cut into
   2.5-cm cubes

3 tsp salt

3 Tbsp basic *rempah* (see page 10)

2 Tbsp curry powder

1 tsp sugar

720 ml water

4 potatoes, peeled and quartered
   then soak in water

240 ml thick coconut milk

1. In a bowl, marinate beef with 1 tsp salt for 10 minutes.

2. Heat a deep non-stick pot over medium heat. Add *rempah* and fry for 2 minutes.

3. Add curry powder. Fry until fragrant, about 2–3 minutes.

4. Add beef. Stir-fry well until meat changes colour.

5. Add salt, sugar and water. Stir to mix well with *rempah*. Bring to a boil over low heat.

6. When gravy boils, lower heat, cover and simmer. Stir occasionally to prevent meat from sticking to pot.

7. When *meat* is soft, add potatoes and cook until potatoes are tender.

8. Add coconut milk and bring back to a boil. When gravy boils, remove from heat.

9. Dish out and serve.

Pot Roast Beef

Leftovers can be used as sandwich fillings served with either sliced cucumbers or lettuce.

Serves 4–6

1 kg beef knuckle

4 large onions, peeled; 3 sliced,
    1 cut into rings

1 thumb-sized piece ginger, peeled

5 cloves garlic, peeled

oil, as needed

1 tsp salt

1 tsp sugar

1 Tbsp ground black pepper

240 ml dark soy sauce

2 potatoes, peeled and cut into
    thin rounds

2 Tbsp frozen green peas (optional)

720 ml water

1 tomato, washed and cut into
    round slices (optional)

1. Buy beef whole. Wash, drain and pat dry with kitchen towel. Slice off membrane or netted veil with a sharp knife. Pierce meat with a big fork for the seasonings to penetrate.

2. Grind sliced onions, ginger and garlic together in a blender or a food processor until fine.

3. Heat pan. Add 2 Tbsp oil and fry ground ingredients until brown.

4. Marinate beef with fried ingredients, salt, sugar, ground black pepper and dark soy sauce. Rub evenly all over. Set aside for 10 minutes.

5. Fry potatoes in some oil until golden brown. Drain on kitchen towels.

6. Blanch onion rings in hot water for 5 minutes. Drain.

7. If using, blanch green peas in hot water for 2 minutes. Drain.

8. Add 2 Tbsp oil and water to beef in a pot. Bring to a boil over low heat. Lower heat. Turn beef occasionally to ensure even browning. Simmer until meat is tender.

9. Cool beef before slicing. Slice along grain so that meat will not disintegrate. Arrange slices neatly on a serving dish.

10. Reheat gravy before pouring over meat. Garnish with onion rings, tomato and peas, if using.

11. Top with fried potato.

12. Serve.

Seh Bak

This is almost always served as an appetizer or starter with the drinks at Eurasian parties. However, many are happy to have it as their main meal, not bothering with the other food served!

Serves 4–6

250 g lean pork (*twee bak*), washed and drained

6 cloves garlic, peeled and washed

1 thumb-sized piece galangal (*lengkuas*), peeled and smashed

1 thumb-sized piece ginger, peeled and smashed

120 ml sweet soy sauce (*kichap manis*)

1 tsp salt

1 star anise, washed

3-cm cinnamon, washed

oil, as needed

1 onion, peeled and ground

600 ml water

2 hard-boiled eggs, quartered (optional)

1 string small square dried deep-fried bean curd (*tau pok*), halved (optional)

1 cucumber, peeled and cut into bite-sized pieces

oil, as needed

2 fishcakes

2 yam roll (*hei piah*)

2 meat and prawn roll (*ngor hiang*)

2 Tbsp roasted sesame seeds (optional)

a sprig of coriander (*ketumbar*), washed (optional)

Chilli Sauce

1 Tbsp minced garlic

2 Tbsp ground chilli

2 Tbsp sugar

3–4 Tbsp vinegar

3 Tbsp chilli sauce

1. Place pork, garlic, *lengkuas* and ginger in a deep pot.

2. Add sweet soy sauce and salt. Mix well.

3. Add star anise and cinnamon to pot.

4. Heat oil in a pan over medium heat. Fry onion until brown. Add fried onion to pot.

5. Add water and eggs, if using, to pot. Mix well. Cover and simmer over low heat until pork is tender and gravy thickens. Turn pork over occasionally to evenly brown the meat with the sauce. When cooked, remove from gravy and cool. Cut into bite-sized pieces. Reserve gravy.

6. If using, scald *tau pok* with hot water. Drain and squeeze water out of *tau pok*.

7. In the same pan, heat oil over medium heat and fry fishcake, *hei piah* and *ngor hiang* until a little browned. Drain on kitchen towels. Allow fishcake, *hei piah* and *ngor hiang* to cool down before cutting into bite-sized pieces.

8. Prepare chilli sauce. Bring chilli sauce ingredients to a boil in a clean pan over low heat. Lower heat, then simmer for 3 minutes.

9. Remove from heat and allow chilli sauce to cool completely.

10. Place pork in a mixing bowl with *tau pok*, cucumber, fishcake, *hei piah* and *ngor hiang*.

11. Add chilli sauce and reserved gravy. Mix well. Arrange on a serving plate. Place eggs on the plate.

12. Garnish with roasted sesame seeds and coriander leaves, if using.

13. Serve.

Shepherd's Pie

This is a wholesome meal that is a convenient snack for school-going kids. It tastes just as good even when cold. The pies can be packed in aluminium trays and frozen before being baked. To serve, thaw the required amount and bake.

Makes one 10 x 5-cm pie

1 Tbsp oil

1 onion, peeled and diced

1 tsp minced garlic

300 g minced beef, pork or chicken

1 tsp salt

1 tsp sugar

1½ tsp ground black pepper

½ tsp cinnamon powder

300 g frozen mixed vegetables
    or garden peas or sliced canned
    mushrooms (optional)

1 kg potatoes, peeled

1 tsp baking powder

2 Tbsp evaporated milk

2 tsp butter

2 eggs, beaten separately

1. Preheat oven to 200°C.

2. Heat pan with oil over medium heat. Add onion and garlic. Fry until onion softens.

3. Add meat, salt, sugar, 1 tsp ground black pepper and cinnamon powder. Stir to mix well.

4. Add mixed vegetables. Fry for about 2 minutes until vegetables are cooked. Dish onto a 10 x 5-cm baking dish.

5. Boil potatoes for 20–30 minutes until potatoes are soft. Mash with a fork until smooth and does not contain lumps.

6. Add baking powder, evaporated milk, butter, remaining ground black pepper and 1 egg. Mix well.

7. Place mashed potato over cooked meat in baking dish. Cover evenly. Use a plastic sheet or plastic spatula to smoothen surface.

8. Brush remaining egg over surface of pie. Bake in preheated oven at 200°C for 30 minutes until surface is golden brown.

9. Remove from oven.

10. Serve warm.

Mutton Chop Curry Moru

I usually don't fancy mutton so much because of the smell. However if fresh mutton chops are purchased, it makes a world of difference. The smell becomes more tolerable to me. Serve with rice, *roti prata*, *briyani* rice or French loaf and fried brinjals (page 72), sambal *timun* (page 91) or sambal *nanas* (page 88) and fried cutlets.

Serves 4–6

water, as needed

300 g mutton chops

2 tsp salt

3 large onions, peeled

1 thumb-sized piece ginger, peeled

5 cloves garlic, peeled

3 Tbsp curry powder

4 Tbsp water

3 Tbsp oil

a sprig of curry leaf (*daun kari*)

1 tsp sugar

4 potatoes, peeled and quartered

3 limes, cut and squeezed

240 ml thick coconut milk

1 tomato, washed and quartered

1. Bring a pot of water to a boil over low heat. Parboil mutton. Remove scum and drain.

2. Bring another pot of water to a boil over low heat. Add mutton again. Remove and drain mutton. Rub with 1 tsp salt and rinse.

3. Grind onion, ginger and garlic together in a blender or a food processor until fine.

4. Mix curry power with water into a smooth paste.

5. Heat oil in a deep pot over medium heat. Fry ground ingredients until brown. Add curry paste and curry leaves and fry until fragrant.

6. Add mutton. Fry until meat changes colour.

7. Add 720 ml water, remaining salt and sugar. Bring to a boil over low heat. Lower heat and cover pot. Simmer until meat is tender. Stir occasionally to prevent curry from burning at the bottom of the pot.

8. Add potatoes. Cook until potatoes are soft.

9. Add lime juice and thick coconut milk.

10. Add tomato and remove from heat.

11. Dish out and serve.

Seafood

Fish Molee *61*

Fish Curry Pementer *62*

Sambal Udang *65*

Dry Prawn Curry *66*

Prawn Sambal Bostadar *69*

Fish Molee

The *feng* curry powder can be purchased from the *rempah* stalls at most Singapore wet markets. Just ask the rempah man to blend *jintan manis, jintan puteh, ketumbar* and *kunyit.* You can also make your own with the recipe given in the The Basics chapter. Serve with rice, fried salted *ikan sepat* and sambal *belacan.*

Serves 4–6

4 Spanish mackerel fillets, about
   80–100 g each, washed

1 tsp salt

1 aubergine (brinjal), stem removed
   and quartered

2 Tbsp oil

1 onion, peeled

2 cloves garlic, peeled

$^1/_2$ thumb-sized piece ginger, peeled
   and julienned

240 ml water

1 walnut-sized piece tamarind (*assam*),
   mixed with 60 ml water then strained

2 Tbsp *feng rempah* (see page 12)

1 tsp sugar

60 ml thick coconut milk

1 Tbsp vinegar

1. Rub fish with ½ tsp salt. Set aside for 10 minutes.

2. Slit each piece of brinjal across in centre but do not cut through, leaving piece whole. Soak in water.

3. Grind onion and garlic in a blender or a food processor until fine.

4. Heat a pan with 1 Tbsp oil over medium heat. Fry marinated fish until lightly browned. Transfer onto a clean plate.

5. In the same oil, fry brinjal until half-cooked. Dish onto same plate as fish.

6. Heat remaining oil in a small pot over medium heat. Fry ground onion and garlic, and ginger until lightly browned and fragrant.

7. Add *feng rempah* and fry for 1 minute.

8. Add water and *assam* water. Bring to a boil over low heat.

9. Add remaining salt and sugar. Bring back to a boil.

10. Add fried fish and brinjal. Simmer for 5 minutes.

11. Add coconut milk and vinegar. Remove from heat once gravy comes to a boil.

12. Dish out and serve.

Fish Curry Pementer

When I am tired of the usual fish curry, I will prepare this curry as the spices used such as cumin and fennel help spice up the curry and make it more fragrant. Serve with rice, salted egg and fried *kang kong*.

Serves 4–6

200 g Spanish mackerel or stingray, washed and drained

1/2 tsp salt

1 aubergine (brinjal)

3 young lady's fingers

2 Tbsp oil

2 Tbsp standard *rempah* (see page 11)

1/2 tsp cumin (*jintan manis*)

1/2 tsp fennel (*jintan puteh*)

1/2 tsp salt

1 tsp sugar

360 ml water

1 walnut-sized piece tamarind (*assam*), mixed with 60 ml water and strained

1. If using stingray, cut into 8 pieces. Rub with salt.

2. Cut brinjal into 3–4 segments. Cut each segment into 4. Soak in water.

3. Wash lady's fingers. Trim away top and bottom ends. Cut diagonally into 3 pieces.

4. Heat oil in a pot over medium heat. Drain brinjal and fry until half-cooked. Drain.

5. Discard oil and in the same pot, add *rempah* and fry for 1 minute.

6. Add anise and cumin. Fry until fragrant.

7. Add lady's fingers and fry for 3 minutes.

8. Add salt, sugar, water and *assam* water. Bring to a boil over low heat.

9. When gravy boils, add seasoned fish. Cook covered for 5 minutes.

10. Add fried brinjals and cook until vegetables are soft, fish is cooked and consistency of gravy is not too thick nor thin.

11. Dish out and serve.

Sambal Udang

This dish is usually served with *nasi lemak*. My mother would make the special *tie miyak* — lime juice is added to boiled thick coconut milk to curdle it and to pour over the sambal to give it a more 'coconut-y' flavour, enhancing the taste of the sambal. Serve with French loaf, plain rice or *nasi lemak*, and omelette and plain vegetable dishes.

Serves 4–6

250 g medium-sized prawns,
   peeled and deveined

1 tsp sugar

1 Tbsp oil

1 tsp minced garlic

2 Tbsp basic *rempah* (see page 10)

$^1/_2$ tsp salt

1 tsp sugar

3 Tbsp water

4 limes, cut and squeezed

1. Place prawns in a basin and rinse with water twice. Marinate with sugar.

2. Heat oil in a pan over medium heat. Fry prawns until slightly pink and half-cooked. Push to side of pan.

3. Add garlic. Fry until brown.

4. Add *rempah*. Fry for 1 minute. Mix with prawns.

5. Add salt and sugar. Mix well. Add water to prevent *rempah* from burning.

6. Add lime juice. Mix well. Remove from heat.

7. Dish out and serve.

Dry Prawn Curry

When I have little time to spare, I would prepare this dish as it is simple and delicious all in one. Serve with rice, pappadom, any fish curry and plain green vegetables.

Serves 4–6

250 g large prawns

2 Tbsp fish curry powder

40 ml water

1 Tbsp oil

2 shallots, peeled and thinly sliced

2 cloves garlic, peeled and thinly sliced

3.5-cm piece ginger, peeled and julienned

1 tsp mixed spices, rinsed and drained

a sprig of curry leaf (*daun kari*)

$^1/_2$ tsp salt

1 tsp sugar

1 walnut-sized piece tamarind (*assam*),
    mixed with 120 ml water and strained

1. Trim eyes and whiskers of prawns with a pair of scissors. Using a sharp knife, devein prawn, leaving shell intact. Rinse and drain.

2. Mix curry powder with 40 ml water into a smooth paste.

3. Heat oil in a pan over medium heat. When hot, fry shallots, garlic and ginger until brown.

4. Add mixed spices and curry leaves and fry for 1 minute.

5. Add curry powder paste and fry until fragrant. Add salt and sugar.

6. Add prawns and stir-fry for 3 minutes.

7. Add *assam* water and continue cooking until prawns are cooked and gravy is dry.

Prawn Sambal Bostadar

Bostadar means 'slap'. The hotness from the chillies makes one feel as if one has been 'slapped' on the face when too much is consumed! Some prefer this as a sandwich filling rather than the famous dried prawn sambal. Serve with bread or rice and fried fish and fried vegetables.

Serves 4–6

300 g medium-sized prawns, peeled and deveined

1/2 tsp salt

10 shallots, peeled

5 candlenuts (*buah keras*)

1 tsp dried fermented shrimp paste (*belacan*)

1 tsp ground turmeric (*kunyit*)

2 Tbsp oil

5 cloves garlic, peeled and thinly sliced

10–15 green chillies, washed and sliced

1 tsp sugar

120 ml thick coconut milk

1. Place prawns in a basin and rinse with water twice. Marinate with salt.

2. Grind shallots, *buah keras* and *belacan* in a blender or a food processor into a fine paste. Mix with ground turmeric.

3. Heat oil in a pan over medium heat. Fry garlic until golden brown. Drain on kitchen towels.

4. In the same oil, fry ground ingredients until fragrant.

5. Add sliced green chillies. Fry for 1 minute.

6. Add prawns and fry until prawns are cooked.

7. Add sugar and coconut milk. When gravy boils and consistency thickens, remove from heat.

8. Dish onto a serving plate and garnish with fried garlic.

Vegetables

Fried Brinjals 72

Eurasian Cucumber Salad 75

Nyonya Chap Chye 76

Fried Brinjals

This dish is usually served hot with curry dishes.

Serves 4

1 purple or green aubergine
   (brinjal), washed

4 soda biscuits

$^1/_2$ tsp salt

$^1/_2$ tsp sugar

$^1/_2$ tsp ground black pepper

1 egg, beaten

125 ml oil

1. Cut brinjal into 4 segments. Cut each segment into 2. Score cut side of each piece, then soak in water to prevent brinjal from turning colour.

2. Grind soda biscuits finely. Mix with salt, sugar and ground black pepper.

3. Drain brinjals and squeeze out excess water. Brush surface with egg. Coat cut surface with biscuit mixture.

4. Heat oil in a pan over medium heat. Fry brinjal, one piece at a time, on the biscuit-coated side first until golden brown.

5. Turn brinjal over to cook the other side. When skin of brinjal changes colour, it is cooked. Remove from heat.

6. Drain excess oil on kitchen towels.

7. Serve.

Eurasian Cucumber Salad

The mustard in the mayonnaise gives a zing to the taste, to overcome the richness of the dish or '*mata jelak*' as we Eurasians would say it. If you do not like the taste of mayonnaise, you could dress the salad with tomato sauce.

Serves 4–6

1 cucumber, skinned

2 bunches local salad leaves, rinsed
 and separated then soak in chilled water

1 tomato, sliced

1 large onion, peeled and thinly sliced

2 hard-boiled eggs, thinly sliced

2 Tbsp mayonnaise

$1/2$ tsp English mustard powder

1. Use the tines of a fork to make desired designs on the cucumber. Rinse and slice thinly.

2. Drain salad leaves. Shake excess water off and wipe each leaf dry with a kitchen towel.

3. Arrange leaves on a flat serving plate until whole plate is covered.

4. Arrange cucumber over salad leaves. Place tomato and onion over cucumber. Top with eggs.

5. Cover salad with plastic wrap and chill in the refrigerator until ready to serve.

6. Mix mayonnaise with mustard powder. Pour over salad just before serving.

Nyonya Chap Chye

This is usually served with either chicken *buah keluak* (page 28). The dish also goes well when served with sambal *belacan*.

Serves 4–6

100 g medium-sized prawns, peeled (optional)

2$\frac{1}{2}$ tsp sugar

1 Tbsp oil

1 onion, peeled and quartered

1 tsp minced garlic

1 Tbsp preserved soybeans (*taucheo*), pounded

50 g yam bean (*bang kwang*), peeled, halves and thinly sliced (optional)

180 ml water

200 g cabbage, washed and cut into small squares

50 g carrots, julienned

1 hard bean curd (*taukua*), cut into small squares and lightly fried

10 g wood ear fungus (*boh jee*) or dried lily buds (*kim chiam*), soaked

10 g glass vermicelli (*tang hoon*), soaked

10 g dried soybean skin (*taukee*), soaked then break into 5-cm pieces

a sprig of coriander (*ketumbar*)

1. If using, marinate prawns with $\frac{1}{2}$ tsp sugar.
2. Heat oil in a pan over medium heat. When hot, add onion. Fry until it softens. Add garlic, *taucheo* and prawns. Fry for 1 minute.
3. Add *bang kwang*, if using. Fry for 1 minute. Add 60 ml water. Add cabbage, carrots and remaining sugar. Continue frying.
4. Add remaining water to soften vegetables. Add *taukua*, *boh jee* or *kim chiam*, *tang hoon* and *taukee*. Cover and simmer for 3 minutes.
5. Remove from heat. Garnish with coriander leaves before serving.

Rice and Noodles

Mee Siam *80*

Eurasian Nasi Goreng *83*

Eurasian Birthday Mee *84*

Mee Siam

This dish is usually prepared for parties or when we would like to eat something other than rice.

Serves 4–6

1/2 Tbsp salt

2 Tbsp sugar

120 ml water

300 g bean sprouts (*taugeh*)

Rempah

3 onions, peeled

3–4 Tbsp ground chilli

1 Tbsp dried fermented shrimp paste (*belacan*)

100 g dried shrimps, soaked in
   hot water for 5 minutes

Beehoon

2 hard bean curd (*taukua*),
   washed and cut into cubes

5 hard-boiled eggs

10 stalks chives (*koo chye*), washed and
   cut into 2.5-cm lengths

5 limes, washed and halved

1 packet dried Chinese rice vermicelli
   (*bee hoon*)

5 Tbsp oil

Gravy

1 onion, peeled and cut into rings

1 Tbsp tamarind (*assam*) mixed with
   120 ml water and strained

3 Tbsp ground preserved soybeans (*taucheo*)

150 g sugar

1500 ml water

Sambal

2–3 Tbsp ground chilli

1 tsp dried fermented shrimp paste (*belacan*)

2 Tbsp oil

1 onion, peeled and cut into cubes

2 tsp tamarind (*assam*), mixed with
   60 ml water and strained

1/2 tsp salt

3 Tbsp sugar

1. Prepare *rempah*. Grind onions, ground chilli, *belacan* and dried shrimps in a blender or a food processor until fine. Set aside to prepare gravy.

2. Prepare *beehoon*. Drain and grind dried shrimps until fine.

3. Using an egg cutter, cut eggs into thin circles.

4. Soak *beehoon* in water until *beehoon* expands. Drain.

5. Prepare gravy. In a large pot, bring onion, *assam* water, *rempah*, *taucheo*, sugar and water to a boil over low heat. Lower heat, then simmer over low heat for 30 minutes.

6. Heat oil in a pan over medium heat. When hot, fry *taukua* cubes. Drain.

7. In the same oil, fry dried shrimps until fragrant.

8. Add ground ingredients and fry until cooked. Reserve 4 Tbsp for later use.

9. Add salt, sugar and water to pan. Bring to a boil over low heat.

10. When mixture boils, add *bee hoon* and fry until gravy is absorbed.

11. Add *taugeh*. Fry until dry and fluffy.

12. Dish onto a serving plate. Garnish with *fried taukua* and sliced eggs. Top with chives. Arrange limes around the plate.

13. Prepare sambal. Grind chilli with *belacan* in a blender or a food processor until fine.

14. Heat oil in a pan over medium heat. Add onion and fry until soft.

15. Add ground ingredients and fry until fragrant.

16. Add *assam* water, salt and sugar. Simmer until consistency is thick.

17. Place *mee siam beehoon* on individual plates.

18. Pour gravy over and top with 1 tsp or more, if preferred, of sambal.

Eurasian Nasi Goreng

This is usually prepared when there's not enough food to go around or when there's leftover rice.

Serves 4–6

300 g day-old cooked rice

50 g dried shrimps

2 Tbsp oil

1 tsp minced garlic

1 onion, peeled and diced

1 Tbsp ground chilli

1 tsp sugar

1 tsp salt

100 g chicken fillet, washed and drained then cut into very small pieces

2 eggs, beaten

1 Tbsp light soy sauce

2 Tbsp fried shallots

1. Loosen rice to make it grainy.

2. Soak dried shrimps in hot water for 5 minutes. Drain and grind in a blender or a food processor until fine

3. Heat oil in a pan over medium heat. When hot, fry ground prawns for 5 minutes.

4. Add garlic and onion and fry until onion softens.

5. Add ground chilli, sugar, salt and chicken. Fry until chicken is cooked.

6. Add egg and scramble mixture.

7. Add rice and light soy sauce. Fry to mix well until rice is grainy in texture.

8. Dish onto serving plate and garnish with fried shallots.

Eurasian Birthday Mee

We usually prepare this noodles on birthdays as consuming the noodles on that day has a special significance of longevity. When frying, we are not supposed to break the noodles with the spatula so that the person celebrating his or her birthday will have long life. Serve with *sambal nanas* (page 88) or Eurasian *achar* (page 90).

Serves 4–6

300 g yellow egg noodles (mee)

100 g Chinese flowering cabbage (*chye sim*), washed and cut into 7.5-cm lengths

50 g streaky pork, washed

100 g fresh prawns, peeled, leaving tail intact and deveined

1$^{1}/_{2}$ tsp sugar

2 eggs

$^{1}/_{4}$ tsp salt

$^{1}/_{4}$ tsp ground black pepper

2 Tbsp oil

2 Chinese sausage (*lap cheong*), diagonally sliced

1 cucumber, peeled and cut into 3–4 segments

1 onion, peeled and quartered

1 tsp minced garlic

1 Tbsp preserved soybeans (*taucheo*)

100 g bean sprouts (*taugeh*), washed

2 red chillies, diagonally sliced

a sprig of coriander (*ketumbar*), washed

2 Tbsp fried shallots

1. Loosen noodles and rinse in a colander. Drain.

2. Slice *chye sim* stems into thin strips.

3. Parboil pork in boiling water for 10 minutes. Remove to cool before slicing into thin strips. Reserve pork stock for later use.

4. Wash and drain prawns. Marinate with $^{1}/_{2}$ tsp sugar.

5. Beat eggs with salt, ground black pepper and 1 Tbsp oil. Heat a wok over medium heat. Fry into an omelette.

6. Allow omelette to cool down before slicing thinly.

7. In the same wok, fry *lap cheong* until light brown. Remove from heat. Set aside.

8. Using a sharp knife slice around the cucumber thinly, in one continuous piece. Discard seeds. Roll cucumber and slice thinly.

9. Heat remaining oil in a pan over medium heat. Add onion and garlic. Fry until brown.

10. Add prawns and fry until prawns change colour.

11. Add *taucheo* and fry for 1 minute.

12. Add remaining sugar, reserved pork stock and sliced pork. When gravy boils, add *chye sim* and *taugeh*. Fry for 1 minute.

13. Add noodles. Fry to mix well until noodles are cooked. Do not overcook vegetables. Add more stock if you feel that the noodles are too dry.

14. Dish onto a serving plate. Garnish first with *lap cheong*, sliced omelette, cucumber, red chillies, fried shallots and coriander leaves.

Achars and Sambals

Sambal Nanas *88*

Salted Fish Pickle *89*

Eurasian Achar *90*

Sambal Timun *91*

Sambal Nanas

Serves 4–6

1 small ripe Mauritius pineapple,
   skinned and washed

100 g cucumber, washed

2 Tbsp sambal *belacan*

2 Tbsp dark soy sauce

3 Tbsp sugar

1. Cut pineapple into 4. Remove core. Cut into small pieces, each about 0.5-cm. Drain.

2. Remove ends of cucumber. Cut into small pieces, each about 0.5-cm. Drain.

3. Mix pineapple and cucumber with sambal *belacan*, dark soy sauce and sugar. Mix well.

4. Transfer to a serving bowl. Chill in the refrigerator for 30 minutes before serving.

5. The sambal will keep for about 1–2 days refrigerated.

Salted Fish Pickle

Serves 4–6

7 Tbsp oil

200 g salted threadfin (*ikan kurau*),
   washed and cut into small pieces

1 Tbsp mustard seeds, soaked
   in hot water

3 Tbsp ground chilli

3 thumb-sized pieces ginger, peeled

3 Tbsp vinegar

3–4 Tbsp sugar + more if needed

1. Heat 4 Tbsp oil in a pan over medium heat.
   Fry threadfin until golden brown.

2. Blend mustard seeds with ground chilli and
   ginger in a blender or a food processor until
   fine.

3. In the same pan, heat remaining oil. Fry
   ground ingredients until fragrant.

4. Add vinegar and sugar. Simmer until sambal
   is almost dry.

5. Cool completely before adding fried salted fish.

6. Store in a clean, dry bottle. The pickle will keep
   for about 5–6 months refrigerated.

Eurasian Achar

Serves 4–6

2 cucumbers, ends removed

10 green chillies

20 shallots, peeled

8 cabbage leaves, cut into
   bite-sized pieces

10 cloves garlic, peeled and sliced

2 thumb-sized pieces ginger,
   peeled and julienned

3 Tbsp oil

$\frac{1}{2}$ tsp mustard powder or paste

2 Tbsp ground turmeric (*kunyit*)

500 ml vinegar

8–10 Tbsp sugar

2 tsp minced garlic

1. Cut cucumbers into 3–4 segments. Cut each segment into 2. Cut each half into 3. Remove core. Drain and use a muslin cloth to squeeze out excess water. Repeat process 2–3 times.

2. Wash green chillies. Pat dry with a cloth. Slit each chilli lengthwise keeping it whole at the stem.

3. Blanch shallots in hot water for 5 minutes. Drain and dry with kitchen towels.

4. Blanch cabbage in hot water. Drain and pat dry with kitchen towels.

5. Heat oil in a wok over medium heat. When hot enough, fry garlic slices until brown. Remove from pan and set aside.

6. In the same pan and oil, fry ginger until brown. Remove from pan and set aside.

7. In the same pan and oil, fry minced garlic until brown. Add mustard and ground turmeric. Fry for 1 minute.

8. Add vinegar and sugar and bring to a boil over low heat. Remove from heat and cool mixture completely in an earthen pot.

9. Add the rest of the ingredients, one at a time, mixing well with a dry porcelain spoon.

10. Pickle for at least 1 day before serving. The *achar* will keep for about 3–4 months refrigerated.

Sambal Timun

Serves 4–6

1 cucumber, halved lengthwise

1 white onion, peeled and thinly sliced

50 g dried shrimps, soaked in hot water
   for 2 minutes

1 Tbsp sambal *belacan*

2 Tbsp vinegar

3 Tbsp sugar

1. Cut cucumber into 2.5-cm pieces diagonally. Arrange neatly on a plate

2. Place sliced onion on top of cucumbers.

3. Using a mortar and pestle, pound dried shrimps coarsely.

4. Mix shrimps with sambal *belacan*, vinegar and sugar. Stir until sugar dissolves.

5. Pour mixture over cucumber to pickle slightly before serving.

Snacks, Cakes and Desserts

Pineapple Tarts

I add butter to the pineapple jam for a smoother texture. You can use store-bought pineapple jam if you don't want to go through the hassle of making your own.

Makes about 80 tarts

1 egg, beaten lightly

Pineapple Jam

5 ripe Mauritius pineapples, peeled and washed

1 cinnamon stick

1 star anise,

2 cloves

300–400 g sugar

2 Tbsp butter

Dough

500 g plain (all-purpose) flour

1 tsp baking powder

1 egg

1/2 tsp salt

3 Tbsp boiled cooled water

250 g butter, softened at room temperature

1. Prepare pineapple jam. Blend pineapple finely in an electric blender. Drain ground pineapple until dry.

2. Cook drained pineapple with spices over low heat until mixture is completely dry.

3. Add sugar. Mix. Cook until sugar dissolves and mixture is dry.

4. Add butter. Mix. Cool completely before removing spices. Use as required. This can be prepared 1–2 weeks in advance. Cool completely before storing in a dry container. Keep refrigerated.

5. Preheat oven to 200°C. Line baking tray with baking paper. Set aside.

6. Prepare dough. Mix flour with baking powder in a bowl.

7. Break in egg. Mix until mixture is crumbly.

8. Dissolve salt in water. Add to flour and mix well.

9. Add butter. Mix until dough is well blended and does not stick to the sides of the bowl. Set aside for 5 hours or overnight.

10. Pinch off some dough and place on a plastic sheet. Cover with another plastic sheet and flatten with a rolling pin until dough is about 2-cm thick. Using a pineapple pastry cutter, cut tarts out. Repeat process until you have about 80 tarts. Roll up excess dough. Cover with a damp cloth so that dough will not dry up.

11. Place tarts on prepared tray. Brush sides of tarts with egg wash. Reserve egg wash for later.

12. Pinch some pineapple jam and roll smoothly on palm into a ball. Place on tart and press lightly to fill tart.

13. Pinch off some excess dough. Flatten with thumb and index finger before cutting into 3 thin strips. Make a leaf design on top of each tart. Brush with remaining egg wash.

14. Bake in oven at 200°C for 20–30 minutes until tarts turn light brown.

Sister Dot's Coconut Candy

I have been making candy for many years and found the following tips helpful for good candy. Some of these tips include using only young white coconut— choose coconut with a lighter brown skin to be grated and using powdered milk for a creamier taste. As the colour of the milk is white, it will not affect the colour of the candy. Keep a separate bottle of diluted red food colouring for the soft pink colour that makes the candy attractive. For bazaar sales, line a box or paper cup with a paper doily before packing the dried candies. You can make either pink or chocolate candy with this recipe.

Makes 60 pieces

2–3 Tbsp full cream powdered milk

125 ml hot water or evaporated milk

2–3 Tbsp cocoa powder (optional)

6 ml hot water (optional)

900 g grated young white coconut

700 g coarse sugar

1 rounded dessertspoon butter or margarine

3–4 pandan leaves (*daun pandan*) or 2 tsp vanilla essence

a few drops of red food colouring

1. Mix powdered milk with hot water in a heatproof bowl.

2. If making chocolate candy, dissolve cocoa powder in water. Add milk mixture to cocoa paste.

3. In a wok, mix coconut and sugar with your hands until well blended.

4. Add milk mixture, butter and pandan leaves or vanilla essence. Mix with wooden spoon until well blended.

5. Cook over high heat until mixture starts to boil. Lower heat, stirring continuously until mixture thickens. Add red food colouring, if making pink candy, and mix well.

6. Remove from heat when mixture starts to dry at the sides of the wok. Dish out immediately onto a board or tray.

7. Using a fork and knife, spread coconut out evenly. Use knife to press sides and fork to press top down. Do not smoothen top with a knife as a good candy should have a rough, coconut texture on top and be moist inside. Allow candy to set for 2–3 hours then cut into pieces. Leave to dry or fan gently if candy is still too moist.

Sesagoon

When I was a child, this was always the first treat to be prepared for Christmas and the last to be eaten, about 2 weeks after Christmas when we had eaten the rest of our treats. We were always advised not to talk while eating it as we might choke or worse still, cough it out onto someone's face! It was made in a *grainseng* (brass pan) over a charcoal fire and coconut shell ladles were used to remove the lumps in the floor. My mother was one of the few people who used to prepare this treat every year. She would store the *sesagoon* in whisky or brandy bottles sealed with a white cloth tied around the cap. *Kapor* is the lime paste Indians and Bibiks eat with betel nut. It can be bought from Indian stores. Substitute with alkaline water if unavailable. Serve *sesagoon* in paper cones for children or with a cup of plain tea.

Serves 10

A pinch of lime paste (*kapor*)
   or 2 Tbsp alkaline water

1 Tbsp water

200 g rice flour

1 egg

$1/2$ coconut, skinned and grated
   or 200 g grated white coconut

$1/2$ tsp salt

1 pandan leaf (*daun pandan*),
   cut into 4 pieces

100 g fine sugar

1. In a bowl, mix lime paste with water into a smooth paste.

2. Mix flour with egg until mixture is crumbly.

3. Add coconut, salt and lime paste liquid. Mix. Add 2 pieces of pandan leaf and stir well.

4. Heat a non-stick pan. Add $1/4$ flour mixture and fry with a wooden spoon. Flatten out lumps and fry until evenly brown.

5. When mixture is golden brown, remove from heat. Allow mixture to cool in a bowl. Repeat the frying process with remaining flour mixture in small batches.

6. When mixture is completely cooled, use a mill to grind until mixture is fine and resembles sand.

7. Return milled mixture to pan and fry over very low heat. Add remaining pandan leaves and fry for about 5 minutes until fragrant.

8. Add fine sugar. Stir-fry until well blended. Cool completely before storing in a clean dry bottle.

Hot Cross Buns

Hot cross buns are usually prepared and served on Good Friday.

Makes 20 buns

500 g bread flour + more if needed

50 g sugar

5 g salt

5 g skimmed milk powder

1 tsp mixed spices

5g bread improver

10 g dry yeast

40 g butter, softened +
   more if needed

290 ml water + more if needed

125 g mixed fruits

1 egg, beaten

1. Preheat oven to 200°C.

2. Place bread flour, sugar, salt, milk powder, bread improver, dry yeast and butter in a mixing bowl. Mix for 1 minute.

3. Add water and mix until dough is formed. Add butter and beat until gluten develops. After about 5–6 minutes. Pinch some dough and stretch until you see a thin film which does not break through.

4. Add mixed fruits. Knead into dough, making sure fruits are well distributed.

5. Remove dough from mixer and place on floured surface. Allow dough to rest for 10 minutes.

6. Portion dough into 20 pieces, each about 40 g. Mould it until gluten is tighten.

7. Roll each piece into a smooth ball. Place buns on baking tray, spaced apart, to allow room for expansion. Set aside to prove for 45 minutes before baking.

8. Add flour and butter together and mix with water until consistency is right.

9. Spoon into a piping bag with a small nozzle. Pipe a cross over each bun. Brush surface of bun with egg wash. Bake in oven at 200°C for 10 minutes in oven until golden brown.

10. Remove from oven. Serve with butter.

Sugee Cake

This is the typical Eurasian wedding cake. Keep the cake refrigerated to preserve the cake. The cake should be fully thawed before eating. Buy ready-made marzipan from bakery shops or supermarkets.

Makes four 17.5 x 9-cm loaf tins

4–5 Tbsp apricot jam

ready-made marzipan

Batter
750 g butter

400 g semolina

15 egg yolks

480 g fine sugar

4 Tbsp flour

6 tsp baking powder

7 egg whites

250 g ground almonds

1 tsp vanilla essence

1 Tbsp brandy

Icing
2 Tbsp lemon juice

1 egg white

500 g icing sugar, sifted

1 tsp glycerine

1. Prepare batter. Melt butter over low heat. When melted, add semolina. Stir and set aside for 5 hours or overnight.
2. Preheat oven to 150°C. Line four 17.5 x 9-cm aluminum loaf tins with greaseproof paper.
3. Beat egg yolks and sugar in a bowl until sugar dissolves and mixture is stiff and white.
4. Sift flour and baking powder together.
5. Whisk egg whites until stiff.
6. Add semolina mixture to yolks and sugar, a little at a time, alternating with ground almonds until batter is well blended.
7. Add sifted flour. Mix well.
8. Add whisked egg whites to batter.
9. Add vanilla essence and brandy.
10. Pour batter into lined tins. Bake in oven at 150°C for 1 hour or until a wooden skewer inserted in centre of cake comes out clean
11. Prepare icing. In a bowl, whisk lemon juice with egg white.
12. Add sifted icing sugar to lemon mixture, a little at a time, until well mixed.
13. Add glycerine. Mix thoroughly. Make sure texture is firm and not runny. If mixture is too thin, add more icing sugar.
14. When cake is completely cooled, gently turn out of tin. Brush with apricot jam.
15. Cut required amount of marzipan. Place on plastic sheet and cover with another plastic sheet. Flatten with a rolling pin to required thickness. Make sure marzipan is larger than cake to be covered.
16. Remove top plastic sheet. Cover cake with marzipan. Press lightly to ensure marzipan is stuck to the cake. Gently remove plastic sheet. Trim excess marzipan from cake with a sharp knife. Make sure cake is completely covered with marzipan. Cake crumbs will stick to the icing if cake is not completely covered.
17. Plaster cake with icing using a spatula. Level icing by running the spatula in egg white. Leave to dry thoroughly before cutting into individual pieces and wrapping in foil to be boxed.

Rich Fruit Cake

Ideally, this cake should be made 1–2 months before eating to allow the cake to mature well. If that is not possible, wait for at least 7 days.

Makes five 17.5 x 9-cm loaf tins

1 kg dried mixed fruits

200 g chopped or sliced almonds

125 ml brandy

450 g plain (all-purpose) flour

$^1/_2$ tsp fine salt

$^1/_2$ tsp all spice

400 g butter, softened

400 g brown sugar

1 tsp vanilla essence

1 tsp rose essence (*ayer mawar*)

7 eggs

1. Soak fruits and nuts in brandy overnight.
2. Preheat oven to 150°C.
3. In a bowl, sift flour with salt and all spice.
4. Cream butter with sugar until light and fluffy. Add vanilla essence and *ayer mawar*.
5. Beat in eggs, one at a time, with a little flour to prevent curdling.
6. Fold in flour and fruit and nut mixture, alternating between the two until batter is well blended.
7. Pour batter into a 25-cm square cake tin and smoothen top. Make a slight dip in centre for a flat cake.
8. Bake in oven at 150°C for 1 hour. Lower temperature to 100°C and bake for another 3–3$^1/_2$ hours. Test with a skewer to ensure cake is done.
9. Leave to cool in tin. When completely cooled, turn cake out and wrap in silver foil.

Banana Cake

I just love the scent of the bananas and the light airy texture of the cake. One of my favourite picks for afternoon tea!

Makes five 17.5 x 9-cm loaf tins

450 g plain (all-purpose) flour

2 tsp baking powder

2 tsp bicarbonate of soda

$^1/_2$ tsp salt

360 g butter, softened

360 g fine sugar

1 Tbsp rum

4 eggs

7 Del Monte bananas, peeled and mashed

4 Tbsp evaporated milk

1. Preheat oven to 150°C. Grease a 30-cm square baking tin. Set aside.

2. Sift flour with baking powder, bicarbonate of soda and salt in a large bowl.

3. In a bowl, cream butter and sugar until light and fluffy. Add rum.

4. Add eggs, one at a time, mixing each time until batter is well mixed.

5. Fold in sifted flour, a little at a time.

6. Add mashed bananas and mix well. Add evaporated milk.

7. Pour batter into greased baking tin. Bake in oven at 150°C for $1^1/_4$ hours until cake is done. Test with a skewer.

8. Remove from oven. Cut into desired number of slices.

Kueh Kochi Coconut

This is a traditional snack made especially for Maundy Thursday. My mum would soak the glutinous rice the Monday before. The next day, it was sent to the soy bean maker to be ground into wet glutinous rice flour. The ground flour was then placed in a cloth bag to drain overnight. By Wednesday morning, the flour would be dry. It was then removed from the cloth bag, seasoned and mixed with coconut milk. The filling and banana leaves would also be prepared at the same time. We still make this *kueh* for sale at St Joseph's Church canteen every Maundy Thursday. Although this *kueh* has the same name as the Malay dessert, there are subtle differences between the two—the Malay *kueh* is white with a brown coconut filling while the Eurasian version is blue and white with a white coconut filling.

Makes 25–30 *kuehs*

Coconut Filling

2 Tbsp cornflour

3 Tbsp water

1 young coconut or 400–450 g skinned
   white grated coconut, grated

1 pandan leaf (*daun pandan*),
   rinsed and knotted

300 g sugar

Dough

300 g glutinous rice flour

1 Tbsp sugar

1 tsp salt

120 ml thick coconut milk

240 ml water + more as needed

$1/2$ tsp blue food colouring

9 banana leaves

oil, as needed

1. Prepare coconut filling. In a bowl, mix cornflour with water.

2. Mix coconut, pandan leaf and sugar in a pot. Cook over low heat.

3. When coconut is cooked and sugar melted, add cornflour mixture to thicken.

4. Cool completely before forming into small balls, each about 10 g. This can be prepared 1–2 days in advance. Store in a covered container in the chiller compartment of the refrigerator.

5. Prepare dough. In a bowl, mix glutinous rice flour with sugar and salt. Mix well. Divide into 2 equal portions.

6. Mix coconut milk with water. Divide into 2 equal portions. Add blue food colouring to 1 portion. Mix well.

7. Add plain coconut milk, a little at a time, to 1 portion of flour until a firm dough is formed. If there is any coconut milk left over, set aside. Do likewise with blue-coloured coconut milk and other portion of flour. If dough is too dry, a little water may be added.

8. Cut each banana leaf into 4 segments. Cut each segment into a strip about 25-cm long with rounded edges. Use the softer portion of the leaf.

9. Scald banana leaves in hot water for 5 minutes to soften. Drain and wipe dry. The leaves can be prepared in advance. Wrap in newspaper and refrigerate to keep fresh.

10. Take one strip of banana leaf, dull side facing up. Rub with oil.

11. Pinch off 10–15 g dough. Flatten with fingers on leaf.

12. Place a ball of cocount filling in the centre. Pinch off 10–15 g blue dough to flatten and cover filling. Bring both doughs together and form into a ball.

13. Place *kueh* in the centre of banana leaf and roll leaf around *kueh*. Pleat one end of leaf and fold in. Repeat the process for the other end.

14. Bring water in a steamer to a rapid boil. Steam *kueh* for 10–15 minutes.

15. The *kueh* will keep for about 1 week refrigerated.

Kueh Kochi Pulot Hitam

This is a uniquely Eurasian *kueh*. A mixture of black and white glutinous rice flour is used for a soft *kueh*. If only black glutinous rice flour is used, the *kueh* will be very hard. We used to grind our own flour from soaked glutinous rice but now it can be bought. The black glutinous rice flour is available in Malacca while the best white glutinous rice flour to use is Elephant brand from Thailand. The *kueh* can be filled with either mung bean or coconut (see *kueh kochi* coconut). Wrap the two fillings in different ways— either in a cone or in the same style as a *nasi lemak* packet. One tip is to wrap the *kueh* in advance and to steam them as and when required. Uncooked *kueh* can be kept for about 3–4 days refrigerated. Another tip is not to over-steam the *kueh* as the banana leaves will turn dull green or even black.

Makes 50 *kuehs*

250 g black glutinous rice flour

500 g white glutinous rice flour

1 Tbsp sugar

$1/2$ Tbsp salt

720 ml water + more as needed

240 ml thick coconut milk

11–12 banana leaves, cut into 4 strips

oil, as needed

Mung Bean Filling

water, as needed

400 g skinned mung beans (*kacang hijau*), washed and soaked overnight

1 pandan leaf (*daun pandan*)

300 g sugar

60 ml oil

1. Prepare mung bean filling. Bring water to a boil in a steamer over low heat. Line steaming tray with a cheesecloth.

2. Drain expanded *kacang hijau* and place on cloth. Using the back of a wooden spoon, make indentations. Top with pandan leaf.

3. Steam for 1 hour until beans are soft. While still hot, mash with a potato masher.

4. Mix mashed beans with sugar in a pot. Cook over low heat until dry.

5. Add oil and mix well. Cool. When cool, form into small balls, each about 10 g.

6. Mix black glutinous rice flour and white glutinous white flour with sugar and salt in a basin.

7. Mix water with thick coconut milk. Add to flour, a little at a time, until a soft dough is formed.

8. Using a pair of scissors, cut top and bottom edges of banana leaf strips into rounded ends.

9. Scald leaves in hot water for 5 minutes to soften. Drain and wipe dry with a cloth.

10. Take a banana leaf strip, dull side facing up. Oil leaf.

11. Pinch off 15 g dough. Flatten onto banana leaf strip.

12. Place a ball of mung bean filling on dough.

13. Seal mung bean filling with dough and wrap inwards with leaf into a cone.

14. Bring water in a steamer to a rapid boil. Steam *kueh* for 15–20 minutes. The *kueh* will keep for about 1 week refrigerated.

Apom Berkuah

I always associate this cake with holidaying in Bedok where our extended family used to cramp into two sea-facing bungalows. Every day a Eurasian lady from Katong would come at teatime to sell her famous *apoms*. We would buy all the apoms she brought, testament to how good they were and how much we enjoyed them! The *apom* moulds are made of brass. You may not find them in Singapore but they are easily available in the Bunga Raya area in Malacca, where there are many shops selling different cake moulds. The best brand of rice flour to use is Elephant brand from Thailand. I've tried making this *kueh* with other rice flours but have not obtained the same results as I do when I use this particular brand. You also need coconut water for this recipe. It helps with the fermentation process and can be obtained from wet market stalls or provision shops that sell grated coconut.

Makes 50–60 pieces

1–2 drops blue or red food colouring

oil, as needed

720 ml water

480 ml thick coconut milk

12 *rajah* or *pisang mas* bananas

Apom

1 packet (500 g) Elephant brand rice flour

2–3 Tbsp glutinous rice flour

2 Tbsp sugar

2 Tbsp dry yeast

250 ml coconut water

500 ml water

250 ml thick coconut milk

1 pandan leaf (*daun pandan*), rinsed

Banana Sauce

240 g palm sugar (*gula Melaka*)

120 g sugar (optional)

120 ml water

3 Tbsp rice flour

60 ml water

2 pandan leaves (*daun pandan*), rinsed and knotted

1. Prepare *apom*. In a bowl, mix rice flour and glutinous rice flour together.

2. Add sugar, dry yeast and coconut water. Mix well.

3. Add water and thick coconut milk. Set aside to ferment for about 1 hour, or overnight in the refrigerator.

4. Wrap pandan leaf round a wooden chopstick.

5. Add food colouring to 1 cup of batter. Mix thoroughly. Leave rest of batter plain.

6. Over an open flame, heat *apom* mould. Grease with pandan leaf dipped in oil.

7. When mould is hot, pour plain batter until about three-quarters full. Add few drops coloured batter.

8. Heat *apom* over low heat until holes appear and *apom* is cooked. Remove from mould and repeat with rest of batter.

9. Prepare banana sauce. Boil *gula Melaka*, sugar and water over low heat until sugars dissolve. Strain. Add sugar only if you prefer the sauce to be sweeter.

10. In a mixing bowl, mix rice flour with water into a smooth paste.

11. Bring syrup and water to a boil over low heat. Add rice flour mixture to thicken.

12. When mixture boils, add thick coconut milk. Bring back to a boil and remove from heat immediately.

13. Peel bananas and slice directly into hot sauce

14. To serve, place *apom* on a saucer and top with banana sauce.

Pulot Urap

During my school days, this were some of the tea treats which my mother would prepare for us for afternoon tea. She would prepare something different everyday and we always look forward to the surprises in store for us!

Makes 30 pieces

1 kg glutinous rice (*pulot*),
  washed and soaked for 1 hour

1 pandan leaf (*daun pandan*),
  rinsed and knotted

240 ml thick coconut milk

2 Tbsp sugar

2 tsp salt

gula melaka syrup, as needed

Steamed Grated Coconut

1 coconut, skinned and grated or
  400–450 g white grated coconut

$^1/_2$ tsp salt

1 pandan leaf (*daun pandan*),
  rinsed and knotted

1. Bring water to a boil in a steamer over low heat. Line steaming tray with a cheesecloth.

2. Drain *pulot* and place in tray. Using the back of a wooden spoon, press rice to compact. Top with pandan leaf.

3. Steam *pulot* for 20–30 minutes. Remove from heat.

4. Prepare steamed grated coconut. Mix coconut with salt. Steam with pandan leaf for 10 minutes. This will prevent coconut from turning rancid. Set aside to cool.

5. Mix thick coconut milk, sugar and salt in a big mixing bowl. Add steamed rice and mix well.

6. Return *pulot* to steaming tray and press to compact. Steam for 5 minutes.

7. While *pulot* is still hot, shape into round balls, each about 30–35 g. Compress balls firmly to give *pulot* a firm texture. Place inside a plastic bag to keep warm.

8. Roll glutinous rice balls in steamed grated coconut.

9. Serve with melted *gula* melaka syrup.

Pulot Tekan With Tartal

This *pulot* dish can be served with either *tartal* (coconut sauce) or *kaya*. When I was a child, my mother had a special wooden tub to compress and turn the *pulot* out easily. Without the tub, my mother flatly refuses to make this *kueh*. She would also always insist on making her own blue colouring from *bunga telang*, a wild flower that used to be easily found. This was a tedious process. The flowers were usually plucked in the morning. The stems were then removed and the flowers dried in the sun till completely dry. They were then stored in a dry bottle for later use. To extract the colour, a handful of dried flowers were boiled in some coconut milk for a beautiful violet shade. Now, for convenience, blue food colouring is used.

Makes 40 pieces

Glutinous Rice

water, as needed

1 kg glutinous rice (*pulot*), washed and soaked for 1 hour

2 pandan leaves (*daun pandan*), rinsed and halved

240 ml thick coconut milk

2 Tbsp sugar

2 tsp salt

½ tsp blue food colouring

banana leaf

Tartal

3 Tbsp rice flour or cornflour

780 ml water

2 tsp salt

1 pandan leaf (*daun pandan*)

240 ml thick coconut milk

Kaya

10 eggs

500 g sugar

240 ml thick coconut milk

1 tsp yellow food colouring

1 pandan leaf (*daun pandan*), rinsed and knotted

1. Prepare glutinous rice. Bring water to a boil in a steamer. Line steaming tray with a cheesecloth.

2. Drain *pulot* and place in tray. Using the back of a wooden spoon, press rice firmly to compact. Top with pandan leaves and steam for 20–30 minutes.

3. Mix thick coconut milk with sugar and salt. Divide into 2 equal portions. Add blue colouring to 1 portion. Mix well.

4. Divide steamed *pulot* into 2 portions. Mix 1 portion with white coconut milk mixture and the other with blue coconut milk mixture. Mix well.

5. Return seasoned *pulot* to steamer. Place coloured rice side by side, keeping them separate. Press rice firmly to compact. Steam for 5 minutes.

6. Arrange coloured rice on a 20-cm tray, one layer at a time, until rice is used up.

7. Use banana leaf to press rice down. Level surface. Cover, turn container over and turn rice out. Place into tray again. Repeat process of pressing rice down with banana leaf.

8. Level surface and cover when cool. Do not cover while rice is still hot as condensation will spoil the appearance of the *kueh* and may even cause it to turn rancid.

9. Cool completely before cutting into 3 x 4-cm squares with an oiled knife. Cut in a straight motion to give an even appearance to the *kueh*.

10. Prepare *tartal*. In a bowl, mix rice flour or cornflour with 60 ml water until a smooth paste is obtained.

11. Bring remaining water, salt and pandan leaf to a boil in a pot. Add rice flour mixture to thicken.

12. Add thick coconut milk. Remove from heat as soon as sauce comes to a boil.

13. Prepare *kaya*. Beat eggs with sugar in a basin or a large bowl. Whisk until sugar melts.

14. Add thick coconut milk and yellow food colouring. Mix thoroughly.

15. Strain into an enamel cup. Place pandan leaf into cup.

16. Bring water to a boil in a steamer over low heat. Place enamel cup in steamer and steam for 1 hour until kaya sets. Cool and store in containers. Spread on *pulot tekan*.

17. Place glutinous rice squares on a plate. Pour sauce over and sprinkle with sugar. You can also serve the *pulot* topped with *kaya*.

Rempah Udang

This used to be served on special occasions such as christening parties. Greasing the leaves helps prevent the leaves from being too dry or brittle. Do not over-bake as the rice will be too hard. Traditionally, the blue colouring was made from the clitoria flower but food colouring is now used. Use strips of foil if banana leaves are unavailable.

Makes 30–35 pieces

oil as needed

Filling

1 coconut, skinned and grated or about 500 g grated coconut

50 g dried shrimps or fresh prawns

120 g shallots, peeled

1 tsp dried fermented shrimp paste (*belacan*)

10 candlenuts (*buah keras*)

2 stalks lemongrass (*serai*), top and two-thirds of roots removed then thinly sliced

2 Tbsp oil

2 Tbsp ground black pepper

1 Tbsp ground coriander

1/2 tsp salt

5 Tbsp sugar

Glutinous Rice

1 kg glutinous rice (*pulot*), washed and soaked for 1 hour

2 pandan leaves (*daun pandan*), rinsed and knotted

120 ml thick coconut milk

1 Tbsp sugar

1/2 Tbsp salt

1/2 tsp blue food colouring

240 ml thick coconut milk, divided into two equal portions

1 Tbsp sugar

1/2 Tbsp salt

40 pieces banana leaves or silver foil, cut into 10 x 15-cm pieces

80 toothpicks, cut into 2

1. Preheat oven to 180°C.

2. Prepare filling. Divide coconut into 2 equal portions. Place 1 portion on a baking tray and bake at 180°C for 10 minutes until coconut is brown.

3. Remove from oven and stir with spoon to make sure coconut is evenly browned. Set aside to cool.

4. When cool, grind in a coffee grinder until fine.

5. If using dried shrimps , grind until fine. If using fresh prawns, mince finely.

6. Bake shallots with *belacan* and *buah keras* at 180°C for 10 minutes until brown and fragrant.

7. Grind *serai* with baked shallots, *belacan* and *buah keras* in a blender or a food processor until fine.

8. Heat oil in a pan over medium heat. When hot, fry ground ingredients until fragrant.

9. Add prawns. Fry for 1 minute. Add toasted coconut. Fry until well mixed.

10. Add ground black pepper, ground coriander, salt and sugar. If you like it sweeter or more spicy, use more sugar or ground black pepper respectively.

11. Stir-fry until mixture is mixed and sugar dissolves. Set aside to cool. The filling can be prepared in advance and refrigerated for later use. Store in a dry container.

12. Prepare glutinous rice. Bring water to a boil in a steamer over low heat. Place a cheesecloth on a steaming tray.

13. Drain *pulot*. Place on steaming tray. Using the back of a spoon, press *pulot* to compact. Top with pandan leaves and steam for 30 minutes.

14. Add sugar, salt and blue food colouring to 1 portion of thick coconut milk. Mix well.

15. Add sugar and salt to the other portion of thick coconut milk. Mix well.

16. Divide the steamed *pulot* into two equal portions. Add one half to the blue coloured mixture. Mix evenly.

17. Add remaining steamed *pulot* to the white coconut mixture. Mix evenly.

18. Preheat oven to 200°C. Grease tray with oil.

19. Line steaming tray with cheesecloth again. Place white *pulot* on one side and blue *pulot* on the other side. Using the back of a spoon, press *pulot* to compact. Steam for 35 minutes until *pulot* is cooked.

20. Scald banana leaves in hot water. Drain and wipe leaves dry with kitchen towels.

21. Place 1 Tbsp white *pulot* on a piece of banana leaf.

22. Add 2 Tbsp filling. Cover with 1 Tbsp blue *pulot*. Press firmly with palm into an elongated shape.

23. Roll banana leaf. Seal ends by folding into a small pleat and fastening with a stapler or toothpick.

24. Arrange wrapped *pulot* on prepared tray. Bake in oven at 200°C for 10 minutes.

25. Remove from oven.

26. Serve warm.

Glossary

Like many Eurasians, and for that matter many Singaporeans, I mix my English with Malay and Chinese dialects-especially when it comes to cooking terms and ingredients.

Assam
Tamarind

Babi panggang
Roast pork

Boh jee
Wood-ear fungus

Buah keluak
Indonesian black nuts

Buah keras
Candlenut (substitute with macadamia nuts)

Chye sim
Chinese flowering cabbage

Gula hitam
Brown sugar

Gula Melaka
Palm sugar

Hei piah
Yam roll

Ikan kurau kering
Salted threadfin

Bang kwang
Yam bean

Bee hoon
Dried Chinese rice
vermicelli

Belacan
Dried fermented
shrimp paste

Belimbing
Sour starfruit (substitute
with tamarind or lemon
juice)

Daun pandan
Pandan leaf

Fishcake

Dried shrimps

Kacang hijau
Green beans or green mung
beans

Ketumbar
Coriander, Chinese
coriander or cilantro

Kiam buay
Preserved plum

Kiam chye
Preserved salted
mustard cabbage

Kim chiam
Lily bud

Koo chye
Chinese or coarse chives. Substitute with
garlic or common chives

Lap cheong
Chinese sausage

Ngor hiang
Meat and prawn roll

Pulot
Glutinous rice

Pulot hitam
Black glutinous rice

Serai
Lemongrass

Tahu
Soft soy bean
cake

Taupok
Dried deep-fried
soy bean

Taukua
Hard soy bean
cake

Taukee
Dried soy bean
skin

Twee bak
Lean pork with skin
(from hind leg)

Limau kasturi
Small limes

Mee
Fresh yellow egg noodles
(substitute with dried wheat
noodles or spaghetti)

**Mustard powder
or paste**
Coleman's powder, Master
Foods or Hreinz paste

Soda biscuits

Tanghoon
Dried mung bean noodles
or glass vermicelli

Taucheo
Preserved soy beans

Taugeh
Beansprouts

Cardamom   **Cinnamon**   **Cloves**

Kunyit
Tumeric

Jintan manis
Cumin

Jintan puteh
Fennel

Mustard seeds

Star anise

Mixed spices
Alba, mustard seeds, fennel and cumin
usually sold premixed in local wet markets

Like many Eurasians, and for that matter many Singaporeans, I mix my English with Malay and Chinese dialects-especially when it comes to cooking terms and ingredients. In fact, Eurasians have their own lingo, which is a mixture of English, Malay, Chinese, Tamil, Portuguese, Dutch and even Arabic. I've spelt these terms as I pronounce them as J feel this best translates the flavour of the book. It will be like I am in your kitchen helping you, as I hope I am. The detailed ingredients list with its photographs and substitutions, where possible, should help you along. Here are translations of some additional terms.

achar	pickle	**nanas**	pineapple
azeti	oil	**nasi**	rice
babi	pork	**pang**	bun
bak	meat	**panggang**	grilled
bendi	lady's fingers	**pementer**	pepper
binagri	vinegar	**pesce**	fish
bostadar	slap	**pikkadel**	cutlet or croquette
brangku	white	**porku**	pork
bredu	vegetables	**rempah**	spice paste
capitan	captain	**roti**	bread
de	of	**sal**	salt
debal	devil	**singgang**	sour-hot
fugar	stir-fried	**soy**	soy sauce
garam	salt	**tambreneu**	tamarind
goreng	fried	**tauyu**	soy sauce
kachang	bean	**tempra**	rempah or spice paste
korku	coconut		
lemak	coconut-y		
limang	lime		
mangga	mango		
masak	cooked		
moru	literally yoghurt but in most cases curry cooked Indian-style		

Index